Road Cycling

The Blue Ridge High Country

ROAD CYCLING
THE BLUE RIDGE HIGH COUNTRY

by Tim Murphy

John F. Blair, Publisher
Winston-Salem, North Carolina

Published by John F. Blair, Publisher

The paper in this book meets the guidelines
for permanence and durability of the
Committee on Production Guidelines for
Book Longevity of the Council on Library Resources

Cover photograph by Tim Murphy

Library of Congress Cataloging-in-Publication Data

Road cycling the Blue Ridge high country / by Tim Murphy.

p.   cm.

ISBN 0-89587-283-8 (alk. paper)

1. Cycling—Blue Ridge Mountains—Guidebooks.   2. Blue Ridge Mountains—
Guidebooks.   I. Title.
GV1045.5.B59M87   2003
796.6'09755—dc21
2003007948

To
Heather

CONTENTS

ACKNOWLEDGMENTS

Many people helped bring this book to life, and I am grateful to them all.

I offer my heartfelt thanks to the folks who helped me develop routes for this book:

R. G. Absher of the United States Army Corps of Engineers, who acquainted me with the route for "The Happy Valley Tour" during an Overmountain Victory Trail cycling event

Shaw Brown of Boone Bike and Touring, who suggested the route for "The Beech Ball Loop"

Michael Davis of the Bicycle Inn in Bakersville, North Carolina, who proposed the basic design of "A Climb to Cloudland: The Roan Mountain Tour"

Matt Daye, who shared the "Glade Valley" route with me, and left me in the dust for most of it

Tom Horsch of Adventure Damascus, who contributed the route for "The Shady Valley Sojourn" and offered valuable advice on the route for "The Road to Damascus"

Scott Warren of Magic Cycles in Boone, who shared the route for "The Bulldog's Bite Loop"

Gary Wyatt, for his patient leadership during a grueling group ride to the top of Mount Mitchell

My thanks also go to the creators of the Blood, Sweat and Gears; Blue Ridge Brutal 100; Bridge-To-Bridge Incredible Challenge; and Rides Around Wilkes (RAW) road-cycling events. These events feature imaginative and challenging routes that have served as the inspiration for several of the rides in this book. These and many other High Country road-cycling events are listed in Appendix D. Come ride them if you can.

I first cycled "The Valle Crucis Loop" during a ride to benefit Peter Congelosi, a beloved employee of Rock & Roll Sports in Boone. Peter lost a valiant battle against cancer in October 2000. I appreciate the members of the Boone biking community who generously gave of their time to organize this special ride.

I extend hearty thanks to Lee McMillan of Shatley Springs Inn for his willingness to allow cyclists to use the inn as a base for "Fountain of Youth: The Shatley Springs Tour." Thanks also go to Allen and Sandra Hincher of Windy Gap Vineyards, who have agreed to host cyclists riding "The Moonshine and Wine Tour."

A tip of the helmet goes to all my good friends in the Brushy Mountain Cyclists Club. Lonny Bumgarner, Nick Cheek, Brandon Eller, Skip Erb, Richard Fink, Jim Hutchens, Sam Hutchens, Bailey Koch, Dwight Levi, Christie Scott, Mike Smithey, Bruce Watts, and Gary Wyatt accompanied me on many of the rides included in this book. Several of them kindly agreed to have their Lycra-clad physiques splashed across these pages. I am especially grateful to Dwight and Jim for their encouragement, their amusing antics, and their willingness to hit the road with me. We've ridden thousands of miles together, and I look forward to many more.

I appreciate the confidence and support of Carolyn Sakowski and all the good folks at John F. Blair, Publisher. This project was the best excuse to ride I could ever imagine.

I owe a huge debt to my wife, Heather, and my children, Kevin, Michael, and Megan. They've put up with me while I've hogged the computer, while I've rolled out weekend after weekend on rides, and whenever I've disappeared into a writer's trance. I hope I can support them in the pursuit of their dreams as they've supported me in mine.

To me, the Blue Ridge is truly God's country. I offer thanks to the good Lord for my health, my family, and these inspiring hills.

Field and forest along the South Fork of the Holston River, from the "Road to Damascus" ride

INTRODUCTION

After cancer, superstar Lance Armstrong was burned out on cycling.

In January 1998, Armstrong moved to Europe to train with the U.S. Postal pro cycling team, hoping to regain his form after treatment for the testicular cancer that almost took his life.

"I was riding with buried doubts, and some buried resentments, too," Armstrong recalls in his autobiography, *It's Not About the Bike: My Journey Back to Life*. Some less-than-stellar finishes in early-spring European races sent Armstrong into a tailspin. He quit the U.S. Postal team, flew home to Texas, and became a self-described bum who drank too much beer, ate too much Mexican food, and channel-surfed his way through the day.

Armstrong might still be on the couch today, a forgotten footnote in the history of sports, if it weren't for his visit to the Blue Ridge High Country.

In April 1998, Armstrong, overweight and out of shape, traveled to Boone, North Carolina, in a last-ditch effort to get his cycling career back on track. With the help of riding buddy Bob Roll and coach Chris Carmichael, he threw himself into riding. "All we did is eat, sleep and ride bikes," Armstrong writes. Through fog and chilly rains, he attacked the rugged hills of the High Country, regaining his fitness and his confidence. In a grueling climb to the top of frosty Beech Mountain, Armstrong found his form mentally and physically.

He took the summit of Beech a restored man. "I was a bike racer again," Armstrong writes of his peak experience. "I passed the rest of the trip in a state of near-reverence for those beautiful, peaceful, soulful mountains. The rides were demanding and quiet, and I rode with a pure love of the bike, until Boone began to feel like the Holy Land to me, a place I had come to on a pilgrimage. If I ever have any serious problems again, I know that I will go back to Boone and find an answer. I got my life back on those rides."

From the depths of despair and disease, Armstrong rebounded to win the Tour de France four years in a row and become the world's top endurance athlete. And his renaissance as a rider began in the North Carolina mountains.

In the Blue Ridge High Country, road cyclists can find natural beauty, challenging climbs, and exhilarating descents for their own peak experiences. "The western part of North Carolina is simply some of the best road riding in the world," *Bicycling* magazine said in March 2001. The 470-mile Blue Ridge Parkway bisects the area, and the hills are laced with a network of paved, low-traffic back roads that offer both inspiring scenery and rugged terrain. With its weathered barns, log cabins, and old country stores, the countryside sometimes looks like the land that time forgot. But a few miles away in Boone and Blowing Rock, great restaurants and a variety of accommodations pamper visitors.

Bike racing hasn't attained the popularity of NASCAR in the Blue Ridge High Country, but the area does have its chapter in American cycling history. Some of the world's best riders raced through the region in the Tour DuPont in the mid-1990s. Several routes in this book retrace portions of those classic tours.

The Blue Ridge High Country is the mountain and foothills region centered on Boone, located in the northwestern corner of North Carolina. The dominant landform here is the Blue Ridge, the front range of the Appalachian Mountains. The Blue Ridge runs northeast to southwest from Pennsylvania to Georgia, attaining its highest elevations in the North Carolina High Country.

There's tremendous variety in the road-cycling options in the Blue Ridge High Country. The terrain on the rides varies from nearly flat to almost wall-like. Elevations range from 6,630 feet above sea level to just under 1,000 feet. Whether you're looking for an easy family spin or a stout ride to test your limits, you can find it in this unique part of America.

It's Different Up Here: The Blue Ridge High Country

The Blue Ridge High Country is a special place with its own weather, natural environment, and culture. It's not like Tallahassee or Terre Haute.

The area has long drawn folks from the flatlands in search of "mountain air." The climate atop the Blue Ridge can both pamper and punish cyclists.

What makes the weather in the mountains so different?

IT'S COOLER

Air generally cools about three degrees Fahrenheit with every 1,000 feet of elevation. On a summer day when it's sizzling in Atlanta or Raleigh, it can be pretty pleasant at 3,300 feet in Boone and maybe even a bit chilly 5,500 feet above sea level atop Beech Mountain. In winter, on the other hand, a day that is ridable in the lowlands can be raw and bitterly cold in the high mountains. Down in the valleys—said to be "so deep you have to pipe in sunshine"—tall mountain walls limit the sun's rays, creating pockets of cool air and making the days seem shorter.

IT'S WETTER

When air rises over the furrowed peaks of the Blue Ridge, it cools and often sheds its moisture. Blowing Rock, one of the High Country's wettest spots, gets an average of 66 inches of precipitation per year. That's about a third more wet stuff than towns in the foothills, just a short drive below. You're more likely to encounter fog, too. Sometimes, fog forms in the cool bottom lands along rivers and creeks. Other times, low clouds enshroud the ridge tops while the valleys below are clear. You can literally climb into the clouds here.

U.S. 221 near Grandfather, from the "Grandfather Mountain Tour"

It's windier

A near-constant summer breeze stirs the air and keeps things comfortable during the year's longest days. Those same winds aren't so welcome in the winter, as they sharpen the chill and swirl savagely, making riding a bike a delicate balancing act. The varied terrain of the mountains tends to channel wind through gaps. The Blue Ridge is notched by scores of these low points in the mountain wall. The early settlers, noting how the gaps channeled the wind, gave them names like Windy Gap and Air Bellows Gap.

The rhythm of the seasons is different in the mountains, too.

SPRING COMES LATER

While the azaleas are in bloom and the air is warm as a friendly hug along the Atlantic in Charleston, it can be gray and chilly in Boone, with just a brave crocus or two to lend hope that winter's end is near. Spring's late arrival in the mountains has its advantages, though. A Southern spring means daffodils, dogwoods, and a green-gold burst of color as the trees revive. It's beautiful but all too short. By visiting the mountains, you can "rewind" spring and enjoy it all over again. Temperatures lag behind those in the lowlands. Highs typically hit the low 70s in the Piedmont in April, but it's not until May that the average temperature is 70 in Boone. Of course, averages don't mean a lot during spring, as the weather is famously variable then.

SUMMER IS COOLER

Average summer high temperatures are in the 70s atop the Blue Ridge. Afternoon rains aren't uncommon. Haze often obscures the view. It can get sticky but is rarely sweltering. July atop the Blue Ridge can feel like May "down the mountain." Rhododendron and wildflowers brighten the landscape, and mountain breezes stir the warm air. Summer is a sweet season on the Blue Ridge.

FALL COMES EARLIER

Not only can you "rewind" spring, you can also "fast-forward" fall. Want to see fall colors and feel some crisp air weeks sooner than you would in the flatlands? Atop the loftier peaks of the High Country, leaves begin to change in late September. In the mountain valleys, mid-October is the trees' time to shine. In the foothills, Halloween usually marks the color peak. Normally the High Country's driest season, fall offers many days of blue skies, moderate temperatures, and expansive views.

Winter is longer

Atop the Blue Ridge, it gets cold sooner and stays cold longer than in the Piedmont. Snow and ice become concerns for cyclists. Winter temperatures swing wildly, depending on whether the weather is coming from the warm Atlantic or the cold interior of the continent. Winter riding requires careful planning and the right clothing, but it has its rewards. Winter's crisp, clear air and bare forests make for excellent views, and tourist-oriented roads like the Blue Ridge Parkway are practically deserted. The foothills offer a variety of challenging, scenic, and lightly traveled routes with weather conditions more conducive to winter cycling.

Conditions in the High Country can be unpredictable. Check the weather before you head to the mountains. Appendix B lists several weather links. The National Weather Service websites offer forecasts that include predicted temperatures and wind speeds for different times of day, which may prove helpful when you're planning what to wear. Booneweather.com offers real-time temperature and wind readings at several points in the High Country.

And if you don't like the weather, stick around anyway—it'll change!

The Mountain Environment

The Blue Ridge Mountains are ancient. They were already eroding when the Rockies, Andes, and Alps were born. A billion years ago, molten magma solidified to form the core of the Blue Ridge. For the next 500 million years, rock was folded, uplifted, and exposed in some spots. Eons of water runoff carved the mountains' pattern of ridges and valleys. Glaciers didn't reach this far south, making the high mountains a haven for Northern plant and animal species displaced by ice.

You'll see a lot of green during summer in the mountains. The forests here are home to more species of trees than all of northern Europe. The highest slopes have been called "islands in the sky." They feature a spruce-fir canopy more commonly found in Canada. Naturalist John Muir summed up the Appalachian forests this way: "They must have been a delight to God because they were the best he ever planted."

The area is also renowned for its flowering trees and plants. In spinning through what ecologists call "edge habitats," cyclists get to see many of them at no extra charge. Spring brings dogwoods and redbuds. Summer is colorful; wildflowers like fire pinks, bee balm, and black-eyed Susans cover the ditches, and two species of rhododendron stagger their blooming seasons along the roadsides from June through August. In early fall, the big weeds take center stage, as towering, 10-foot-tall ironweed and joe-pye weed inhabit roadside fields.

Traveling quickly and quietly through edge habitats, cyclists have the element of surprise on their side in their encounters with the animal world. I've biked around a bend to encounter a vacillating deer that saw me, stepped left, stepped right, then finally bounded off, not quite knowing what to make of me. I've pedaled past a red-tailed hawk swooping down to snatch a small rabbit out of a ditch. I've whipped around a downhill curve at 40 miles per hour to come face to face with a buzzard flapping furiously to get out of my way; my path led straight through its dining room, where it had been enjoying some road kill moments earlier. Strangest of all, a buddy and I once saw a bobcat bound across the Blue Ridge Parkway in broad daylight. We looked at each other to make sure we weren't hallucinating, for bobcats are normally shy and nocturnal denizens of the deep woods. So be alert—you're not alone out there.

Mountain People

While biking the back roads of the Blue Ridge, cyclists get a slow-motion glimpse of mountain life.

This is an area that entered the 20th century late. Electricity reached some back areas of the mountains only after World War II. The spring box inevitably gave way to the refrigerator, and the fiddle and banjo to radio and later television. Yet the old ways hang on here.

The area's isolation demands self-reliance. As you ride through the mountains in the warm months, you'll see homes flanked by vegetable gardens, bee stands, and trees sagging with fruit. Though a lot of folks living in the country now work in town, many maintain the ability to provide for themselves, which harks back to the days when "you raised what you ate and you ate what you raised," as the saying goes. The deer hunter, the trout fisherman, and the kids picking blackberries on the side of the road all are making the most of what the mountains provide.

Signs of modern life aren't hard to find: satellite dishes, double-wide trailers, and the same fast-food restaurants found anywhere in the United States. Yet you can pedal around a bend and still find homegrown acoustic music, cluttered, creaky country stores, and hearty food fit for a farm hand. It's a place of contradictions, as the old ways compete with the new but stubbornly refuse to die.

Faith is important here. Many of the first settlers were religious dissenters fleeing the notion that someone else could tell them how to worship. You'll see churches everywhere you ride in the High Country, even way back in the most sparsely populated areas. And you'll observe that they're unfailingly well kept. Many of the churches offer "salvation by signboard" through posted admonitions for sinners. "The church," Senator Sam Ervin once said, "won't keep you from sinning, but it'll keep you from enjoying your sin."

Like cyclists, mountain folks have a love of the outdoors. "If I had to go into a city and live, I'd soon die," an elderly mountain woman told author Warren Moore. "I just want to be left in the mountains and be quiet and be left alone and be free." Hunting, fishing, and gardening are a few of the ways mountain people keep their connection to the natural world.

And please allow me to puncture the myth of the malevolent mountaineer. Like many other American subcultures, mountain folks have been stereotyped. This prejudice sometimes seeps into magazine articles and Internet postings on cycling in the southern Appalachians, leading people outside the area to believe that the byways of the Blue Ridge are home to rampaging rednecks intent on doing bodily harm to any cyclists unfortunate enough to be in their paths.

Fear not. Over decades of road riding in the area, I have found the vast majority of motorists to be safe and considerate. Driver inattention and miscalculation, not road rage, usually are at the root of the few car-bike mishaps that do occur.

YOUR BIKE AND GEAR

The 26 rides in this book are all on paved roads, except for about a half-mile of dirt road in the 800-plus miles of routes covered. Road bikes are the ideal bicycles for these routes. They're lighter, roll easier, and offer more varied and more aerodynamic riding positions than their off-road cousins. That's not to say that mountain bikes and hybrid bikes have no place on the highways of the High Country. Thanks to hybrids, cross bikes, and mountain bikes, you have the option of exploring the many miles of unpaved roads that crisscross the Blue Ridge. Just don't count on going as far or as fast as you could on a road bike.

Whatever type of bike you ride, be sure it's in good condition before you hit the hills. Steep terrain isn't just rough on riders; it's brutal for bikes, too.

The mountains ask a lot of your brakes. On steep switchbacks, sheer stopping power is important. So is your ability to modulate your brakes. Check cables, calipers, and pads for smooth, even brake operation. But don't go overboard with the cable tension; the last thing you want on a grinding uphill is a binding brake.

Out of the shade, into the sun, from the Boone Back Roads Loop

Gravel, potholes, and some really fast descents are inevitable in the mountains. Don't push your luck. Good tires properly inflated will not only prevent punctures, they'll keep you safe as you push your bike to the limit.

Shifters, derailleurs, cranks, cassettes, and chains all get a workout. You'll shift a *lot* in the mountains. It's not uncommon to go all the way from your top gear as you scream down a long hill to your lowest gear as you chug your way up the next grade. When you're slogging up a steep slope, a skipping, stubborn, slow-shifting drive train can be extremely irritating. Tune your drive train and save your annoyance for the tourists in the turquoise Winnebago.

And speaking of gearing, just how low a gear will you need to cycle successfully in the High Country? The answer depends on your level of cycling power. Superfit, 5,000-mile-a-year riders can get by with rear cassettes the size of corncobs. These titans of the tarmac can power up any hill, albeit with tremendous pressure on the knees. Then there are the well-fed desk jockeys who pedal for fun and fitness. No one will confuse these average Joes and Jills with Lance Armstrong, but using lower gearing, they can slowly spin up hills on which their superfit buddies may have to grind. Be realistic in reckoning your fitness. It's frustrating to run out of gears before you run out of hill.

If you're just visiting the mountains, retrofitting your road bike with a triple crank just to get a few lower gears isn't the way to go. It's an expensive modification and complicates your shifting patterns. Going with a wider-range cassette is a simpler and less costly option. Shimano makes road cassettes up to 27 teeth; Campagnolo cassettes are available with 29.

If, on the other hand, you are (or aspire to be) a frequent Blue Ridge biker, a triple crank may be for you. A triple crank (or "granny gear") is a third, smaller-sized front chain ring. A triple gives you knee-friendly "bail-out" gears for those truly wicked ascents. The ultrafit purists on their high-geared racing rigs will glance at you disdainfully, but let's face it, they were probably looking at you like that anyway. A triple will give you the option to climb almost anything.

Many of the routes in this book will take you miles from civilization, so be a good Scout and bring a pump, a tube, patches, and a multi-tool. A LED flasher may come in handy when fog or mist is likely. Just don't go overboard stuffing the bike bag. Bulky bikes are crummy climbers.

If you plan to mix hiking with your biking, bring a lock. There are plenty of opportunities to stretch your legs off the bike along these routes, if you're so inclined. Some High Country road riders use mountain-bike pedals on their road bikes, since it's easier to walk in mountain-bike shoes.

As for clothing, keep the High Country's famously variable weather in mind as you plan. If you're traveling to the mountains to ride, stuff your duffel with all your riding duds and make your final clothing decisions after you arrive. A perfectly balmy spring day in the Piedmont can be cool and blustery on the Blue Ridge Parkway. Layers are good. Find some cyclists starting a High Country ride early on a frosty fall morning and you'll see precious little exposed skin. But follow them as the sun gets high and you'll see so much stripping that you'll think it's happy hour at the Kit-Kat Klub. Polypropylene skullcaps, glove liners, leg warmers, and arm warmers are functional and easy to carry, making them handy pieces for riding in the transitional seasons.

Remember, there is one must-wear apparel item no matter the weather: a properly fitted bicycle helmet.

Safety

A great ride is a safe ride. Here are some tips on how to stay safe as you bike the Blue Ridge.

Avoid high-traffic routes. Except as noted in the individual ride descriptions, the routes in this book are relatively low in traffic. U.S. 321, U.S. 421 and N.C. 105 near Boone are all high-traffic routes and should be avoided, especially on weekends. Traffic on the Blue Ridge Parkway can vary tremendously according to the day, time of day, and season. The section of the parkway between Blowing Rock and U.S. 421 sees a good deal of local traffic.

Read the road carefully. Pavement conditions vary from the usually smooth Blue Ridge Parkway to the rough surfaces common on many secondary roads. The roads here are generally in decent repair, but given the extremes of mountain weather, expect occasional potholes. Except for parts of the town of Boone, you won't find wide shoulders or designated bike lanes. In downhills, look out for gravel and slag in curves, especially after heavy rains.

Make sure you're seen. Curves and terrain limit drivers' sight distance. Colorful clothing and, in foggy conditions, LED flashers and reflective gear will help drivers notice you. Always ride defensively. Sometimes, that means riding farther out in the lane than normal in curves to make sure you're easily visible.

Descend safely. Speeds of 50 miles per hour and more are possible on downhills. Before you let 'er rip, be sure your brakes are fine-tuned and your tires are properly inflated and in good condition. As you descend, watch for road hazards and debris, but don't focus on them; always look where you want the bike to go. Your position on the bike makes a difference. Slide back on the saddle and position your hands in the drops in case you need the brakes. If you're going too fast, sit up and let wind resistance help slow you down. To promote traction in curves, extend your outside leg and weight the outside pedal forcefully.

Protect yourself. Always wear a properly fitted

helmet approved for bicycle use. Impact-resistant shades are also a great idea, as you never know when you'll come face to face with the hard exoskeleton of an errant insect. Some mountain canines have developed a taste for the well-toned calves of cyclists; some mountain cyclists have begun carrying dog repellent spray as a countermeasure. Carry identification and any important medical information, just in case.

Obey the law. In North Carolina, Tennessee, and Virginia, the bicycle has the legal status of a vehicle. Cyclists have full rights and responsibilities on the roadway and are subject to the same regulations as motor-vehicle operators. State traffic rules require cyclists to ride on the right in the same direction as other traffic, to obey all traffic signs and signals, and to use hand signals to communicate intended movements. All cyclists under age 16 on public roads in North Carolina and under age 12 in Tennessee must wear bicycle helmets. The Blue Ridge Parkway requires cyclists to ride single file to the right of the traffic lane. Bikes are prohibited on all parkway paths and trails. Both state and parkway regulations require headlamps and reflectors at night and during periods of low visibility.

Call if you need help. Use 911 to contact emergency services. On the Blue Ridge Parkway, call 800-PARKWATCH.

Planning Your Ride

About half the rides in the book begin within 10 miles or so of Boone, with the rest spread out across seven counties in

North Carolina, Virginia, and Tennessee. The rides are grouped into general geographical categories beginning with the Boone area and proceeding in a rough clockwise fashion from there.

If you're driving in for just the day, you'll do more riding and less driving if you pick a ride that starts near your edge of the High Country. Most of the start sites are parks or other public areas where parking is no problem. A few of the rides don't have public parking; be sure to ask permission before using any private parking areas. When parking along the Blue Ridge Parkway, don't block gated areas, and never leave your car overnight.

The rides range from 11 to 62 miles. Mountain miles can be a lot more grueling than flatland miles, so adjust your mileage expectations accordingly. For riders who just can't get enough, several of the routes include optional extensions.

Each route description lists the food and services available along the way; it is noted when food and water are hard to find on particular rides. Most community stores and cafés are open year-round. Many tourist-oriented facilities on or adjacent to the Blue Ridge Parkway shut down from November to April.

The high and low elevations are listed for each ride. These elevation spreads suggest the range of temperatures you may encounter, an important consideration in cool weather. In summer, high-elevation rides are the most comfortable. In winter, foothills rides are the best bets.

If you want to get a pack of cyclists arguing, ask them at the end of a ride how tough it was. The route one rider rates as a death march might feel like a Sunday spin to another. The "Challenge" rating listed for each ride is based on several objective factors, including the number, length, and steepness of climbs. Each ride is rated on a three-chain-ring scale.

Ⓓ Rides of one chain ring or less are easy. They're short and have few or no hills. Rides in this category are best for new riders, families, and couples in which one rider is a lot stronger than the other. Gear-shifting technique is not critical on these rides.

ⒹⒹ Rides rated one and a half to two chain rings are tougher. They're longer and feature hills with moderate grades up to a mile or so in length. Fit riders will spend plenty of time in the second chain ring on these rides.

ⒹⒹⒹ Rides rated two and a half to three chain rings are the toughest. They feature multiple climbs, each several miles in length. Some of these climbs can be quite steep, with up to double-digit grades. Riders with triple chain-ring gearing will use their smallest ring on some of these climbs. Some riders without granny gears may wish they had them. If you like to climb, these are the rides for you.

Appendix A lists the rides in order of challenge. You can use it to select the right routes for your level of fitness.

FINDING YOUR WAY

Getting lost is no fun. Here are some tips on how to stay on track as you ride the routes in this book.

Use the mileage listings in the "Cues" section of each ride as a rough guide only. Your observed mileage may vary.

Secondary roads in North Carolina are identified by four-digit S.R. numbers. These numbers are posted vertically on stop-sign posts at intersections, but they're small and easy to miss. Green street signs identifying secondary roads by name are larger and easier to spot, so they're referenced first in the "Cues."

Secondary roads in Virginia are identified by three-digit numbers, usually in the 600s or 700s. These numbers are posted much more prominently than the secondary-route numbers in North Carolina, so they're referenced first in the "Cues."

Secondary roads in Tennessee are identified by name only. Green street signs identify these roads.

"Cues" for rides on the Blue Ridge Parkway refer to the parkway's milepost system. Small concrete posts on the southbound shoulder of the parkway are engraved with mile numbers, running from Milepost 0 at Rockfish Gap, Virginia, to Milepost 469 near Cherokee, North Carolina. The posts are exactly one mile apart, except for the section near Grandfather Mountain. The construction of this section of the parkway was delayed by decades of legal wrangling. When it finally opened in 1987, the "missing link" was 1.2 miles longer than anticipated when the milepost system was developed. Rather than redoing all the mileposts from Blowing Rock to Cherokee, each mile in the new segment was "stretched" to accommodate the extra mileage.

Avoid the temptation to take shortcuts. The hills of the High Country are riddled with roads that dead-end or abruptly turn to dirt. Mountainous terrain can confound even the most intuitive navigator. Unless you're sure where the road goes, you're better off sticking to the "Cues."

If you do get off track, don't panic. Backtrack until you get to a point mentioned in the "Cues." If all else fails, ask for help. Most folks will be more than willing to point you in the right direction. Even the most self-reliant, card-carrying macho man needs help sometimes.

*My heart's in the
Highlands, wherever I go.*

ROBERT BURNS

The Boone-Blowing Rock Area

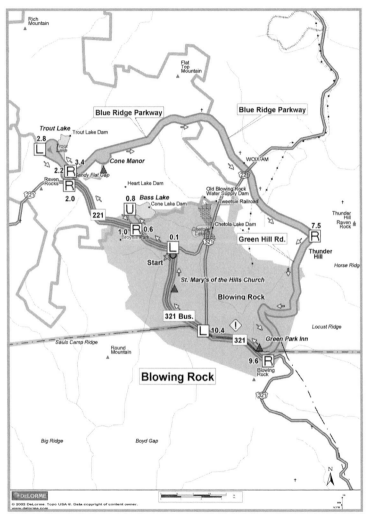

Rich Mountain

Flat Top Mountain

Blue Ridge Parkway

Blue Ridge Parkway

Trout Lake
2.8
L
Trout Lake Dam
WQLX-AM
2.2
R
Sandy Flat Gap
Cone Manor
3.4
221
Raven Rocks
R
Heart Lake Dam
2.0
Old Blowing Rock Water Supply Dam
Thunder Hill
Raven Rock
0.8
U
Bass Lake
Cone Lake Dam
Tweetsie Railroad
221
1.0
R
0.6
Broyhill Park
Chetola Lake Dam
Chetola Lake
7.5
R
Green Hill Rd.
Thunder Hill
0.1
L
321
Start
Horse Ridge
St. Mary's of the Hills Church
Blowing Rock
Locust Ridge
321 Bus.
L
10.4
321
Green Park Inn
Sauls Camp Ridge
Round Mountain
9.6
R
Blowing Rock
Blowing Rock

Big Ridge
Boyd Gap

N

© DeLorme
© 2002 DeLorme. Topo USA ®. Data copyright of content owner.
www.delorme.com

© 2002 DeLorme (www.delorme.com) *Topo USA ® 4.0*

Parkway bridges are works of art.

A MANOR IN THE MOUNTAINS: THE BLOWING ROCK TOUR

SHORT TAKE

You'll tour the toniest town in the Blue Ridge on this 11-mile loop route in and around the resort community of Blowing Rock, North Carolina. The tour offers a look at the manor house and estate of turn-of-the-20th-century "denim king" Moses Cone. It includes a fast descent and a tough climb on the Blue Ridge Parkway and ends with an easy cruise from Thunder Hill down to Blowing Rock's upscale Main Street.

In Depth

If you thought life in the mountains was all about pioneers roughing it in crude log cabins, prepare to see how the other half lived. For over a century, Blowing Rock has been a magnet for magnates, attracting the upper crust with its cool climate and arty ambience. By the 1890s, Blowing Rock's population tripled in the summertime as visitors—mostly New South bankers and industrialists—rode horses, played tennis, bowled, and attended dances and social events.

No one individual made more of a mark on the landscape of today's Blowing Rock than Moses Cone, a textile tycoon who died in 1908. His large estate and his home, Flat Top Manor, flank the town even today. This tour visits several parts of Cone's 3,500-acre estate, but it takes a little imagination to see the place the way it once was. The deer park and the more than 30,000 apple trees from Cone's prizewinning orchard are gone. About half the cleared land has been reclaimed by forest. Cone's house, once the hub of socializing in the area, is now a crafts center, with little to suggest its previous glory.

Cone Manor

Just a mile or so from the hubbub of Main Street in Blowing Rock, the ride stops at the edge of Bass Lake, a 21-acre impoundment Cone stocked with black bass. Ice was cut from Bass Lake in the winter for the manor's refrigeration needs. Today, a broad, flat trail popular with runners surrounds the lake. Cone laced his estate with 25 miles of carriage trails, but don't get tempted; they're all closed to bikes, and offenders must pay hefty fines. Walk down the trail and you'll see Cone's big white manor house on the hill overlooking the lake.

Up the hill and across the Blue Ridge Parkway from Bass Lake is Trout Lake, a peaceful 15-acre pond surrounded by a hemlock-dominated cove forest. Cone stocked it with 8,000 rainbow trout. The flood of 1916 burst the dam and wiped out Trout Lake. It wasn't rebuilt until 1949.

A mile or so up the parkway is Flat Top Manor, Cone's 13,000-square-foot home. Today, the main floor is a crafts center operated by the Southern Highlands Handicraft Guild. The rest of the house is closed to the public. Many of the estate's trails interconnect here, making the manor a popular place for hikers and horse riders. Guests can perch in one of the rockers on the broad front porch and enjoy a commanding view of Bass Lake and the town of Blowing Rock below.

The tour reenters the Blue Ridge Parkway for three miles of classic parkway riding. It's a two-mile downhill glide from the estate to the U.S. 221/U.S. 321 interchange at the bottom of the hill, then a steep pull to the top of Thunder Hill. It's an apt name; Blowing Rock receives more rain and stormy weather than just about any place in the region.

Green Hill Road winds through a forested residential area, giving a glimpse of life in Blowing Rock today. You'll see nice

Green Park Inn

homes, yes, but no 3,500-acre estates; land values are astronomical in today's Blowing Rock.

The route passes the Green Park Inn as it turns onto busy U.S. 321. The inn was built in the same era as Cone's Flat Top Manor. Just imagine riding in a hot train to Lenoir in the foothills below, then bouncing for hours in a horse-drawn coach up the Blue Ridge to this spot. Sometimes, the coaches got mired in mud up to the axles on that rough road. What a welcome sight this fine inn must have been!

The tour ends with a spin down Blowing Rock's Main Street. You'll pass St. Mary's of the Hills Episcopal Church on the right just before entering the business district. If this were Mitford, you could catch Father Tim preaching here on Sunday. Jan Karon, author of the popular Mitford novels, once lived here. She based her fictional small town on Blowing Rock.

Then it's on to downtown, where you can get anything from a ham biscuit to an antique Oriental rug. Folks flock to the park benches overlooking Main Street in the summertime just to watch the parade of people on the sidewalks.

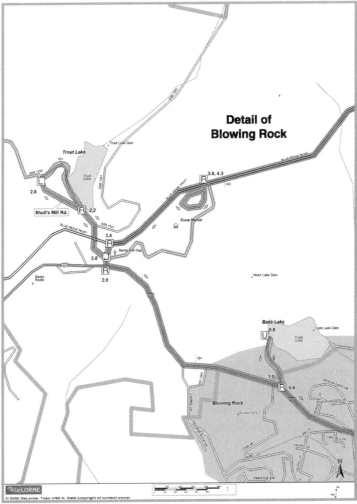

© 2002 DeLorme (www.delorme.com) *Topo USA* ® 4.0

Directions to the Start

Take U.S. 321 Business to downtown Blowing Rock. Turn onto Park Avenue near the Blowing Rock Town Hall. Free parking is available on Park Avenue and near the American Legion hall. The ride begins at the parking area on Park Avenue adjacent to Blowing Rock Town Park.

Distance

11.5 miles

Challenge

⊗⌀ The one-mile climb on the Blue Ridge Parkway from U.S. 221/U.S. 321 to Green Hill Road is this short route's only significant ascent.

Road Conditions and Cautions

The roads on this route are generally smooth surfaced and in good repair. Look out for sections of uneven pavement on the descent from the parkway into Blowing Rock on Green Hill Road. Expect traffic throughout the ride. The three-quarter-mile section of U.S. 321 between the Green Park Inn and Main Street is busy. Parkway regulations require cyclists to ride single file.

CUES

0.0   Turn **left** from Park Avenue onto Main Street.

0.1   Turn **left** at the traffic light onto U.S. 221 South (Yonahlossee Road).

0.6   Turn **right** at the auto entrance to Bass Lake at Moses Cone Park.

0.8   **Turn around** at the parking area for the Bass Lake trailhead. The loop hiking trail around Bass Lake can be accessed here.

1.0   Turn **right** onto U.S. 221 South.

2.0   Turn **right** onto S.R. 1571, a Blue Ridge Parkway access road, then make a **quick left** onto Shull's Mill Road (S.R. 1552).

2.2   Turn **right** onto the unmarked paved drive just past Flannery Fork Road.

2.6   **Loop around** the parking area for the Trout Lake trailhead. The loop hiking trail around Trout Lake can be accessed here.

2.8   Turn **left** at the stop sign onto Shull's Mill Road and head toward the Blue Ridge Parkway.

3.3 Turn **left** at the stop sign onto S.R. 1571, a parkway access road.

3.4 Make a **quick right** at the stop sign onto the Blue Ridge Parkway and head north toward the Moses Cone Estate.

3.9 Turn **right** at the driveway into the Parkway Craft Center at Flat Top Manor.

4.3 Turn **right** at the stop sign from the parking area at the Moses Cone Estate to head north on the Blue Ridge Parkway.

7.5 Turn **right** onto Green Hill Road (S.R. 1534).

9.6 Turn **right** at the stop sign at the Green Park Inn onto U.S. 321 North.

10.4 Turn **left** onto U.S. 321 Business (Main Street).

11.5 Turn **left** onto Park Avenue.

Elevation Profile

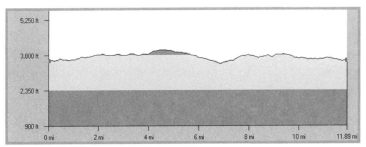

© 2002 DeLorme (www.delorme.com) *Topo USA* ® *4.0*

HIGHEST ELEVATION

3,995 feet just past Flat Top Manor, 4.5 miles into the ride

LOWEST ELEVATION

3,444 feet at the U.S. 221/U.S. 321 overpass, 6.4 miles into the ride

FOOD AND SERVICES

Public restrooms are available at Blowing Rock Town Park and at the carriage house at the Moses Cone Estate. Blowing Rock's Main Street offers a wide variety of restaurants.

ROADSIDE ATTRACTIONS

Seasonal crafts demonstrations are scheduled daily at the Parkway Craft Center, housed in Flat Top Manor, the former home of Moses and Bertha Cone. The Moses Cone Estate is located at Milepost 294 on the Blue Ridge Parkway. For more information, call 828-295-7938.

OUTDOOR OPTIONS

Trout Lake, Bass Lake, and the Moses Cone Estate are laced with more than 20 miles of hiking and equestrian trails. Loop trails around Trout Lake and Bass Lake can be accessed from the parking areas on the route. Bicycles are not allowed on any parkway trails.

High road, low road: the Blue Ridge Parkway's Linn Cove Viaduct towers above U.S. 221.

THE
GRANDFATHER MOUNTAIN TOUR

SHORT TAKE

It's hard to decide what's more impressive. Is it the swooping Linn Cove Viaduct, an engineering marvel opened in 1987? Or is it Grandfather Mountain, a natural marvel that's 600 million years old? No matter. You'll encounter them both on this 21-mile loop. The route climbs the forested lower slopes of Grandfather via U.S. 221, a snaky, shady road tucked between dramatic rock outcrops and cascading mountain creeks. The way back takes you across the acclaimed Linn Cove Viaduct, a land

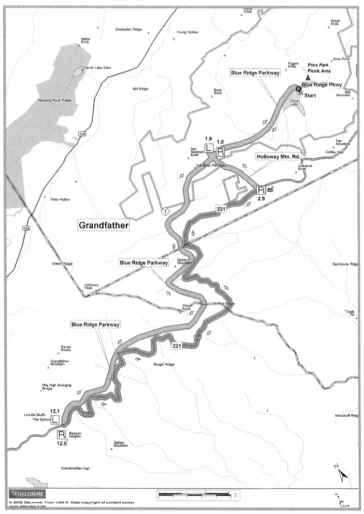

© 2002 DeLorme (www.delorme.com) *Topo USA* ® 4.0

bridge perched on Grandfather's rugged shoulder. The ride ends with a lengthy, thrilling, not-too-technical descent.

In Depth

At 5,964 feet above sea level, Grandfather Mountain truly is the granddaddy of local peaks. It's the tallest mountain in the Blue Ridge, the "front range" of the Appalachians that runs from Pennsylvania to Georgia. It's also the most striking mountain in the High Country, its huge rock crags jutting insolently into the sky. Its jagged profile makes it instantly recognizable even from many miles away.

A dramatic peak deserves a dramatic ride, and this route delivers. It begins at Price Lake, a beautiful impoundment of two small mountain creeks. The ride follows the Blue Ridge Parkway south for about two miles before turning off at Holloway Mountain Road. A mountain bog is visible on the right just off the parkway. Swampy areas are rare in this steep mountain country.

The ride cuts across Holloway Mountain Road to U.S. 221. Until the Blue Ridge Parkway's "missing link" was completed in 1987, all parkway traffic followed this route. U.S. 221 traces the path of the Yonahlossee Trail, blazed by Hugh MacRae in 1889 as a toll road to Linville. Three hundred men worked two years hacking this winding road out of the rocky, densely forested southeastern slope of Grandfather. Visitors paid two dollars a head for a stagecoach ride from Blowing Rock to MacRae's Linville resort.

As the road undulates, it crosses several creeks that cascade toward the Wilson Creek wilderness below. It twists and turns incessantly, flanked by large granite outcrops. The mountain almost seems to swallow riders on this road.

Then, suddenly, around a bend, you'll spy the rocky summit of Grandfather through a gap in the trees, girded by the futuristic-looking Linn Cove Viaduct, the most complicated concrete bridge ever built. You'll be riding across that ribbon of road in the sky soon enough.

At the 12-mile mark, the route leaves the Yonahlossee Trail for the more open Blue Ridge Parkway. The parkway runs a higher route across Grandfather's southeast face. You're above the dense forest now. The wind-whipped trees are shorter, the rock crags more prominent. High on the left is the ridge line of Grandfather, a region author Shepherd Dugger claimed is "as rugged as if Vulcan's mighty anvils had been thrown from the throttles of a volcano and lodged in the mountainside." Grandfather's jagged profile is often shrouded in fog as low clouds bump into this formidable natural obstacle.

Grandfather Mountain, an International Biosphere Preserve, supports 16 distinct ecological communities, including some normally found in Canada. Sometimes called an "island of the North in the South," it is home to 42 rare and endangered species.

Concerns over damage to the fragile mountain environment stalled the construction of this stretch of the parkway for years. The route finally chosen traverses a flank of the mountain covered with large, loose boulders. The viaduct, a quarter-mile-long, S-shaped land bridge, rides over that boulder field. It took three years and nearly $10 million to complete this feat of engineering genius. To protect the terrain, the bridge was built from the top down, eliminating the need for heavy equipment on the ground.

Rocky Grandfather Mountain looms over the Blue Ridge Parkway.

The viaduct consists of 153 uniquely shaped 50-ton segments anchored to seven piers. A trail from the Linn Cove Viaduct Visitor Center goes beneath the viaduct to give an inside view of the components of this award-winning bridge.

The viaduct is best experienced by bike. As you head north across it, the entire horizon to your right will seem to open up, exposing miles of ridges and the vast mountain sky. It feels like you're flying, not riding a bike. On a clear day, it's easy to see why the Cherokees called the Blue Ridge "the unending mountains."

Beyond the viaduct, the parkway hugs the mountain for a few miles. The ride hits its highest elevation, 4,535 feet, just past the viaduct at the Pilot Ridge Overlook.

It's all downhill from Pilot Ridge as you descend a smooth, fairly straight section of the parkway back to Price Lake. Depending upon wind conditions and your bravado, speeds of 50 miles per hour or more are possible here. The parkway flattens past Holloway Mountain Road for a nice cool-down spin to the starting point.

DIRECTIONS TO THE START

From Blowing Rock, take the Blue Ridge Parkway about four miles south to the Price Lake Overlook, Milepost 296.7. A parking lot overlooking the lake is located just off the parkway. Daytime parking is permitted at parkway overlooks and shoulders, but don't block gates or leave your vehicle overnight.

DISTANCE

21.4 miles

CHALLENGE

✪ ✪ There's plenty of climbing on U.S. 221, but it's interspersed with some fairly flat stretches.

ROAD CONDITIONS AND CAUTIONS

The Blue Ridge Parkway and U.S. 221 are smooth surfaced

and well maintained. Parts of U.S. 221 are curvy and offer limited sight distance. Cross winds and fog are possible near the Linn Cove Viaduct on the parkway. Expansion joints on several parkway bridges create sharp bumps. The long, relatively straight descent at the end of the ride can lead to speeds of 50 miles per hour or more. Parkway regulations require cyclists to ride single file.

CUES

0.0 Turn **left** out of the Price Lake Overlook parking lot onto the Blue Ridge Parkway and head south.

1.8 Turn **right** onto the ramp leading to Holloway Mountain Road.

1.9 Turn **left** on Holloway Mountain Road (S.R. 1559).

2.9 Turn **right** at the stop sign onto U.S. 221 South.

12.0 Turn **right** onto the ramp leading to the Blue Ridge Parkway.

12.1 Turn **left** at the stop sign onto the Blue Ridge Parkway and head north.

21.4 The ride ends at the Price Lake Overlook.

Navigation note: The otherwise reliable Blue Ridge Parkway

milepost markers aren't accurate on this stretch of the parkway. When the section from U.S. 221 to Holloway Mountain Road opened in 1987, it was 1.2 miles longer than anticipated when the parkway milepost system was originally planned. Rather than redoing all the mileposts from Blowing Rock to Cherokee, each mile in the new segment was "stretched" slightly to accommodate the extra mileage. That's why the Blue Ridge Parkway is a 470-mile road that ends at Milepost 469.

HIGHEST ELEVATION

4,535 feet 13 miles into the ride, near the Pilot Ridge Overlook

LOWEST ELEVATION

3,380 feet at the start and finish at Price Lake

Elevation Profile

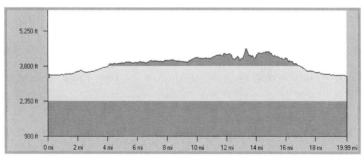

© 2002 DeLorme (www.delorme.com) *Topo USA* ® 4.0

Food and Services

Water and restrooms are available seasonally at the Julian Price Memorial Park picnic area, just north of the start and finish site. The Grandfather Mountain Market is located at the intersection of U.S. 221 and Holloway Mountain Road. Restrooms, water, and visitor information are available at the Linn Cove Viaduct Visitor Center, located at Milepost 304.4, less than a mile after you enter the parkway.

Roadside Attractions

The Linn Cove Viaduct Visitor Center, just off the parkway at Milepost 304.4, offers visitor information, a scale model of the viaduct, and a trail that winds beneath the massive bridge.

Outdoor Options

The 4,300-acre Julian Price Memorial Park offers camping, fishing, hiking, and picnicking. Rental canoes are available at Price Lake. Miles of hiking trails parallel this stretch of the parkway, including the boardwalk portion of the Tanawha Trail, accessed from the Rough Ridge parking area. Bicycles are not allowed on any parkway trails. For more information, call 828-298-0398 or visit www.nps.gov/blri/conepric.htm.

Grandfather Mountain offers spectacular hiking, native animals displayed in natural habitats, and a swinging bridge near the peak. An admission fee is charged. For more information, call 800-468-7325 or visit www.grandfather.com.

Riding toward Grandfather: U.S. 221 at the eastern continental divide

THE VALLE CRUCIS LOOP

SHORT TAKE

This half-century route is a local classic. It begins in a deep valley along the Watauga River and rambles through three North Carolina counties before making a twisting descent back into the peaceful "Valley of the Cross." The ride traverses roads once used by stagecoaches—roads that are seemingly little improved since! More recently, the world's top bike racers screamed through parts of the route during the Tour DuPont.

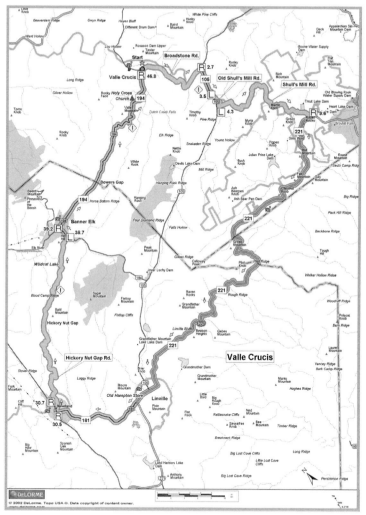

© 2002 DeLorme (www.delorme.com) *Topo USA* ® *4.0*

The Mast General Store, a Valle Crucis mainstay since 1889

In Depth

The ride begins at Valle Crucis Community Park, a pleasant spot along the Watauga River that is perfect for a post-ride picnic. The route follows the Watauga upstream. The stretch along Broadstone Road passes the Mast Farm Inn, an upscale restaurant and bed-and-breakfast that's come a long way since David Mast built a log cabin here in 1812. His humble cabin still stands on the grounds of the inn and is easily visible from the road. The pedaling here is fairly easy, a good warmup for the climbing soon to come.

After a short, unavoidable jog on busy N.C. 105, the route resumes its meander along the Watauga River on Shull's Mill Road. The river provided power for the old gristmill, long since gone, that gave the road its name. Now, the Watauga's highest function is to serve as a summertime swimming hole.

Shull's Mill Road climbs for several miles through a hardwood forest, offering occasional glimpses of Grandfather Mountain. Before the Civil War, stagecoaches traveled this road. The bumps and imperfections will give you a small taste of the rattling that 19th-century travelers routinely endured in those horse-drawn "gut shakers."

Though Shull's Mill Road hasn't changed much, the forest and the surrounding community certainly have. The Whiting Lumber Company logged thousands of acres of old-growth forest in the area during the second decade of the 20th century. The once sleepy community of Shull's Mill had 1,000 residents by 1917, as loggers, sawmill workers, and their families moved in. The lumber boom went bust when the timber was logged out. Today, the area near the old mill is home to a golf course and two upscale communities.

Shull's Mill Road tops out near the Blue Ridge Parkway. The route turns right onto U.S. 221, the old Yonahlossee Trail. This was also once a coach road. Today, it's a smooth-surfaced joy to ride, thanks to its swooping downhill stretches, its shady deep forest, and the repeated glimpses it offers of Grandfather Mountain.

After a long descent to Linville, the character of the route changes. N.C. 181 is a modern road with none of the incessant twists and turns found on U.S. 221. Following a climb to unmarked Montezuma Gap, it's an easy glide into the Avery County seat of Newland.

You'll pass through a few stoplights in Newland, then head back into the woods as the route leaves smooth, broad-shouldered N.C. 181 for the bumpier charms of Hickory Nut Gap Road. You'll climb through a dense oak-hickory forest to the gap. This category-three climb from the 1995 Tour DuPont is steep at the beginning but soon levels out into a gradual uphill where fit riders can pick up some speed. The plunge from the gap into Banner Elk is quite tricky. The road is curvy, rutted, patched, bumpy, and covered with sand and gravel in spots. This is definitely not a descent where you can just let 'er rip. A full-suspension mountain bike wouldn't be a bad idea on this treacherous downhill.

Once you get to Wildcat Lake, a swimming area owned by Lees-McRae College, the road widens and the white-knuckle descent is over. The ride enters Banner Elk, a small town tucked between two massive peaks; Beech Mountain looms over the town at one end, while Grandfather's jagged profile rims it on the other.

The road out of Banner Elk toward Valle Crucis is called the Balm Highway, but this steep creek-side route is more a vexation than a balm. You'll find the Watauga County sign at Bowers Gap a welcome sight, as it marks the end of the last uphill of the ride.

The descent into the "Valley of the Cross" offers inspiring views. Unfortunately, those views occur at spots in the road where you'll be doing your best just to keep your bike between the ditches. A sign at the top of the descent warns large trucks in no uncertain terms to turn back. The narrow road plummets precipitously through curve after curve. One legendary set of switchbacks passes the same house three times! The road quality here is marginal—a little better than Hickory Nut Gap Road, but not much. Look ahead, note the hazards, and then focus on the path where you want your bike to go.

A beautiful Episcopal church will pop up suddenly on the downhill juggernaut. After purchasing 3,000 acres here in 1842,

Climbing past Christmas trees toward Hickory Nut Gap

Bishop Levi Ives instituted a divinity school and a monastic order that were soon forced to disband. Later, the denomination opened a mission school here. Today, the facility is a parish church and diocesan conference center.

The road widens and flattens as it enters Valle Crucis, so known because several creeks converge here to form the shape of a cross. Turn left and you're just a few pedal strokes from "downtown" Valle Crucis and Mast General Store. Turn right and you're back at the start of the ride.

DIRECTIONS TO THE START

From Boone, take N.C. 105 to Broadstone Road (S.R. 1112); the intersection has a traffic signal and a prominent Valle Crucis sign. Turn right on Broadstone Road and proceed 2.7 miles. Turn right onto the gravel access road near the parking lot for the Candy Barrel. A small sign at the head of the drive identifies the area as Valle Crucis Community Park. Leave your vehicle in the parking lot at the park.

Distance

46.8 miles

Challenge

✪✪✪ Patience is a virtue on this ride's long ascents.

Road Conditions and Cautions

The roads on this ride range from smooth and well maintained to bumpy and potentially hazardous. The left turn onto Old Shull's Mill Road from N.C. 105 requires caution, as N.C. 105 is a busy road with many impatient motorists. The descents on Hickory Nut Gap Road and N.C. 194 should be approached with caution, due to rough pavement conditions.

Cues

0.0   Turn **left** out of the dirt driveway from Valle Crucis Community Park onto Broadstone Road (S.R. 1112).

2.7   Turn **right** at the traffic signal onto N.C. 105. Caution: You will likely encounter heavy traffic.

3.5   Turn **left** onto Old Shull's Mill Road (S.R. 1568).

4.3   Turn **left** at the power substation onto Shull's Mill Road (S.R. 1557).

9.6   Turn **right** at the stop sign onto S.R. 1571, a connector to U.S. 221, then make a **quick right** at the stop sign onto U.S. 221 and head south toward Linville.

23.4   Go **straight** at the Blue Ridge Parkway.

26.5   Go **straight** at the N.C. 105 traffic signal in Linville.

27.2   Go **straight** onto N.C. 181 and head north toward Newland.

30.5   Turn **right** onto N.C. 194 North at the traffic signal in Newland.

30.7   Turn **right** at the next traffic signal onto Montezuma Street/Hickory Nut Gap Road (S.R.1342). Follow the double yellow line around the courthouse square.

34.9   You will reach Hickory Nut Gap, elevation 4,333 feet. Caution: You will encounter poor pavement on the descent.

38.7   Turn **left** at the stop sign onto N.C. 184.

39.2   Turn **right** onto N.C. 194 North at the traffic signal in Banner Elk.

Elevation Profile

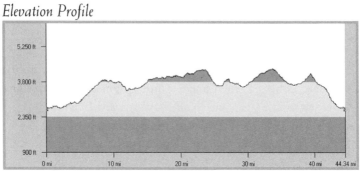

© 2002 DeLorme (www.delorme.com) *Topo USA* ® 4.0

41.3   You will reach Bowers Gap at the Watauga County line, elevation 4,135 feet. A tricky descent begins here.

46.8   Turn **right** at the stop sign onto Broadstone Road. The driveway to the park will be on your left just after the turn.

HIGHEST ELEVATION

4,333 feet at Hickory Nut Gap, 35 miles into the ride

LOWEST ELEVATION

2,670 feet at the start and finish in Valle Crucis

FOOD AND SERVICES

Restrooms are available seasonally at Valle Crucis Community Park. Stores and restaurants are located in Linville, Newland, Banner Elk, and Valle Crucis. The Old Hampton Store and Grist

Mill, just off N.C. 181 in Linville, is a nice place to grab a snack.

ROADSIDE ATTRACTIONS

The Old Hampton Store and Grist Mill, just off N.C. 181 in Linville, is an authentic gristmill that grinds out cornmeal and whole-wheat flour. Its restaurant serves barbecue sandwiches on freshly baked yeast rolls. The mill is open year-round. For more information, call 828-733-5213.

Holy Cross Episcopal Church is located on N.C. 194 in Valle Crucis. Built in 1925, the church is now part of the Valle Crucis Conference Center. It and several other buildings here are listed on the National Register of Historic Places. For more information, call 828-963-4453 or visit www.highsouth.com/vallecrucis.

OUTDOOR OPTIONS

Interested cyclists can enjoy seasonal swimming in the Watauga River and Wildcat Lake.

Grandfather Mountain offers spectacular hiking, native animals displayed in natural habitats, and a swinging bridge near the peak. An admission fee is charged. For more information, call 800-468-7325 or visit www.grandfather.com.

Rolling along Buckeye Road

THE BEECH BALL LOOP

You'll have a ball circling Beech Mountain on this 38-mile loop. Much of the ride winds through dense hardwood forests populated by beeches, buckeyes, sugar maples, and other species normally found farther north. Rushing creeks, green meadows, big views, and the college town of Banner Elk, North Carolina, add variety to this thrill ride through the woods.

SHORT TAKE

This route may be the closest you'll come to a mountain hike on a road bike.

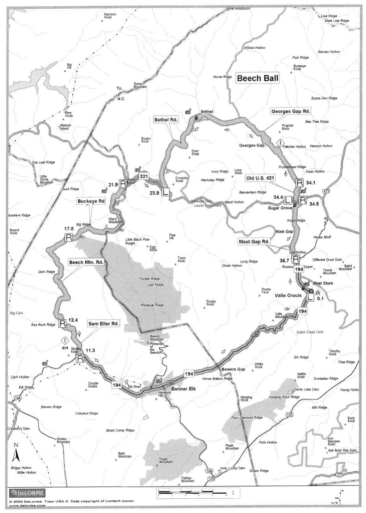

Beech Ball

Bethel Rd.

Georges Gap Rd.

Bethel

Georges Gap

21.9 **R** 321

23.9 **L**

Old U.S. 421

34.1 **R**

Buckeye Rd

34.4 **L**

34.5 **R**

Sugar Grove

17.8 **R**

Mast Gap

Mast Gap Rd.

Beech Mtn. Rd.

36.7 **R**

194

Mast Store

Valle Crucis

0.1 **L**

194

12.4 **R**

Sam Eiler Rd.

dirt 11.3

R

194

Bowers Gap

194

194

Banner Elk

N

© 2002 DeLorme (www.delorme.com) *Topo USA* ® 4.0

In Depth

It follows several winding mountain roads through the woods of Avery and Watauga Counties, revealing parts of the High Country far from the beaten path. At one point on this ride, a buddy of mine stopped at a break in the trees to peer into the pristine valley below. "We're not in the middle of nowhere," he said, "but we're sure on the edge of it."

The route climbs quickly into the woods from the broad, open Watauga River Valley at Valle Crucis. It's a steep, snaky climb on N.C. 194 out of the valley to the Avery County line at unmarked Bowers Gap, elevation 4,135 feet. This category-two climb was a familiar feature on the Tour DuPont.

A descent and some flat pedaling in Banner Elk offer a return to civilization and a respite from climbing. Hulking Beech Mountain looms over the small town, which is home to Lees-McRae College.

Past Banner Elk, N.C. 194 can be annoyingly busy. It's a great relief to leave the hustle of the highway for lonely Sam Eller Road. This country lane winds through the back country of Avery County, passing Christmas-tree farms, backwoods cabins, old barns, and some broad views toward Roan Mountain and Tennessee. Don't panic when the road abruptly turns to dirt; a holdout landowner refused to give the state permission to pave the road. After less than a quarter-mile, you'll be back on blacktop again.

The road climbs more than 800 feet over three miles from the Elk River Valley along the western shoulder of Beech Mountain. The payoff for the climb is a cruise on a gentle downhill through a Northern hardwood forest of beeches, poplars, and sugar maples. Jagged rock outcrops flank the road, and tall trees arch over it. Dappled sunlight occasionally penetrates the tunnel of trees. This stretch is a blazing blur of color in the fall. Riding through the swirl of falling leaves feels like a swift trip through an Impressionist painting.

At Buckeye Road, the route rushes from the ridge back to the valley. The road winds along bold Buckeye Creek, named for the numerous buckeye trees nearby.

After a short stretch on U.S. 321, the ride gets back to the back country with a soaring descent on Bethel Road. The first mile of Bethel Road is wide, smooth, and fast. It's easy to hit speeds of 45 miles per hour or more here. Bethel Road follows Beaverdam Creek up a broad, verdant valley. Stately old farmhouses and rugged barns make the ride into Bethel feel like a trip back in time.

Then it's back into the woods for the ride's last major climb, the short, steep, zigzagging approach to Georges Gap. The dividing line on the wavily surfaced road is as uneven as the road itself. Was the line painter into some white lightning that day,

Bethel is quiet farm country.

or did the paint just slide off the steep slope of the roadbed? It's funny, the things the mind will fixate on to blot out pain.

You'll feel like you've been launched by a slingshot after you crest unmarked Georges Gap and begin the headlong plunge toward Sugar Grove. The road plummets through a succession of tight hairpin curves that are perilously easy to overshoot. The broad vistas only distract from the pressing task of reading the road, choosing a line, braking just enough, and leaning the bike through the turns. The road unkinks at last, and so will you when you can finally let your rig rip without fear of flying off the side of the mountain.

From the edge of nowhere at Sugar Grove, it's just a few short miles back to scenic, sophisticated Valle Crucis and its shops, galleries, restaurants, and inns.

DIRECTIONS TO THE START

From Boone, take N.C. 105 to Broadstone Road (S.R. 1112); the intersection has a traffic signal and a prominent Valle Crucis sign. Turn right on Broadstone Road and proceed 2.7 miles. Turn right onto the gravel access road near the parking lot for the Candy Barrel. A small sign at the head of the drive identifies the area as Valle Crucis Community Park. The ride begins at the parking lot for the park.

DISTANCE

38.2 miles

Challenge

⊛⊛⊄ Georges Gap is the toughest of this ride's three major climbs.

Road Conditions and Cautions

Road surfaces on the route vary widely. A short section of Sam Eller Road is dirt. Much of the route is nearly traffic-free, but the four-mile stretch of N.C. 194 from Banner Elk to Sam Eller Road can be busy. Caution is required on the switchback curves from Georges Gap.

Cues

0.0   Turn **right** out of the dirt driveway from Valle Crucis Community Park onto Broadstone Road (S.R.1112).

0.1   Turn **left** just past a small bridge onto N.C. 194 South.

5.5   You'll reach Bowers Gap at the Avery County line, elevation 4,135 feet. This is the top of the Valle Crucis climb.

7.6   Go **straight** at the traffic signal in Banner Elk.

11.3   Turn **right** onto Sam Eller Road (S.R.1310). The green sign at this intersection says S.R. 1124; the stop sign says S.R. 1310. (If you wish to avoid the 0.2 mile of dirt on Sam Eller Road, stay on N.C. 194 another 1.1 miles and turn right on Beech Mountain Road. You'll reenter the route at the intersection of Sam Eller Road and Beech Mountain Road, noted at mile 13.2 below. This variation adds 2.5 miles to the route.)

12.4   The dirt road begins.

12.6   The dirt road ends.

13.2   Turn **right** at the stop sign. Continue following S.R. 1310 onto unmarked Beech Mountain Road.

14.7   You'll reach an elevation of 4,029 feet at the top of the climb.

14.8   Bear **right** and follow the main road onto unmarked Flat Springs Road (S.R. 1316).

17.8   Turn **right** just before Beech Mountain School onto Buckeye Road (S.R.1312).

21.9   Turn **right** at the stop sign onto U.S. 321 South.

23.9   Turn **left** at the top of the hill onto Bethel Road (S.R. 1202). The green sign at this intersection says S.R. 1202; the stop sign says S.R.1201.

29.2   Go **straight** onto Georges Gap Road (S.R. 1240).

*Cresting
Georges Gap*

31.4   You'll reach Georges Gap, elevation 3,434 feet, where you'll begin a tricky descent.

34.1   Turn **right** at the stop sign onto Old U.S. 421 (S.R. 1233).

34.4   Turn **left** at the stop sign onto U.S. 321 South.

34.5   Turn **right** onto Mast Gap Road (S.R. 1117).

36.7   Turn **right** at the stop sign onto N.C. 194 South.

38.2   Turn **left** into the driveway to Valle Crucis Community Park.

HIGHEST ELEVATION

4,135 feet on N.C. 194 at Bowers Gap, 5.5 miles into the ride

Elevation Profile

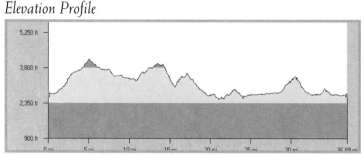

© 2002 DeLorme (www.delorme.com) *Topo USA* ® 4.0

LOWEST ELEVATION

2,508 feet at the Buckeye Creek bridge at U.S. 321 and Buckeye Road, 21.9 miles into the ride

FOODS AND SERVICES

Restrooms are available seasonally at Valle Crucis Community Park. You'll find stores and restaurants in Banner Elk and Valle Crucis; Valle Crucis offers a variety of dining options, from sandwiches and ice-cream cones to gourmet fare. Stores are also located on Buckeye Road, U.S. 321, and Bethel Road.

ROADSIDE ATTRACTIONS

Established in 1883, Mast General Store is listed on the National Register of Historic Places. Clothing, outdoor gear, housewares, and general merchandise are sold in the store, which also houses the community's post office. Mast General Store is located on N.C. 194 in Valle Crucis; for more information, call 828-963-6511 or visit www.mastgeneralstore.com.

N.C. 184 near Beech Mountain—now that's a hairpin curve!

THE BEECH MOUNTAIN CLIMB

SHORT TAKE

You'll trace the tracks of the pros on this short but grueling 22-mile ride. The route features two ranked climbs from the Tour DuPont: a tough, twisting ascent out of Valle Crucis, North Carolina, and a steep, switchback-loaded slog up the storied slopes of Beech Mountain. Three exhilarating descents are the reward for enduring these classic climbs.

IN DEPTH

The crowds and cameras are gone. No helicopters hover in the air. The "Go Lance" signs fans painted on the pavement

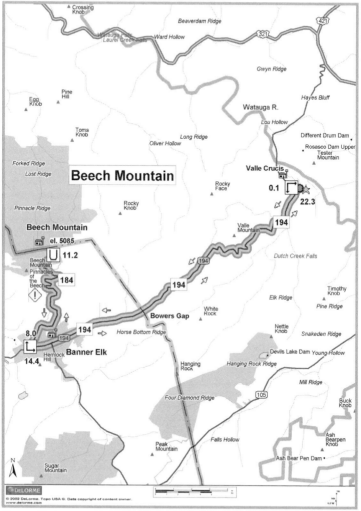

© 2002 DeLorme (www.delorme.com) *Topo USA* ® 4.0

have long since faded. The platoons of world-class riders don't race here anymore, but Beech Mountain is etched in cycling history nonetheless.

Beech Mountain was the showcase climb of the Tour DuPont, America's premier road-cycling event during the 1990s. The Tour DuPont, which ran for the last time in 1996, was the highest-ranked cycling stage race outside Europe. It attracted top riders from around the world, including American legend Greg LeMond and a brash young Texan clawing his way up the pro-cycling ladder, Lance Armstrong.

The tour visited Beech Mountain each year from 1993 to 1996, and Armstrong finished the stage first or second each time. More than 15,000 people lined the final three kilometers near the top of the course, cheering the American as he duked it out against top European competitors like Raul Alcala and Pascal Hervé.

The climb from Banner Elk to the top of Beech Mountain gains 1,450 feet in three miles. It's ranked as a category-one climb, not quite as tough as the *haute catégorie* ascents in the Tour de France, but pretty darn close.

"The climb to the top of Beech Mountain looks and feels like Alpe d'Huez," Tour DuPont winner Viatcheslav Ekimov said in 1994. "It is so steep, especially toward the top."

"Beech is special; it has all the ingredients," Armstrong said after his win at the mountain in 1995. "It's as close as we get to European climbs in this race. It's a classic."

You can't play baseball at Yankee Stadium; you can't buzz your car around the superspeedway at Daytona; and you can't bounce your basketball at Madison Square Garden. But you can experience the climb that drew some of the world's top endurance athletes, and changed one of them forever.

Lance Armstrong's biggest climb up Beech Mountain wasn't his heralded stage win in 1995, but a climb far away from the spotlight during a training ride three years later. Armstrong, depleted by cancer and discouraged by a lackluster return to professional cycling, quit the sport. He returned to the High Country in a last-ditch attempt to resurrect his career. Lance Armstrong regained his form on that trip. He later said the turning point came on a chilly April morning when he got to the top of Beech Mountain.

Before you can have your personal mountaintop moment on Beech, you'll have to climb out of the Watauga River Valley. Snaky, uneven N.C. 194 hugs the side of Valle Mountain as it twists upward through the woods. You'll actually gain more elevation on this climb than on the famed ascent from Banner Elk to Beech, but it's interspersed with a short stretch of flat riding along Crab Orchard Creek near the tiny community of Matney. The climb is a category two—not as tough as Beech, but steep enough to hurt. If you're wiped out by the time you crest unmarked Bowers Gap at the county line, imagine how the Tour DuPont riders must have felt. By the time they got to Bowers Gap in 1994, they already had 120 miles and five categorized climbs under their belts that day.

It's a coast from Bowers Gap at the Avery County line into Banner Elk, a one-stoplight college and resort town. Banner Elk is also the base town for the Beech climb.

It's a scant three miles from the base of the mountain to the stage finish near the Beech Mountain Town Hall, but what a three miles it is! The road is agonizingly steep. At some point during the climb, you're bound to feel like a Wild West gun-

Climbing up Valle Mountain near Matney

slinger trying to fire the seventh shot from his trusty six-shooter. You'll round a hairpin curve, Beech looming above and the road getting steeper. You'll tap your rear derailleur lever to downshift, only to find that the well has gone dry. No more gears means you'll have no choice but to stand on it and hope your noodly legs will make the cranks turn.

Once atop Beech, you can enjoy the view from eastern America's highest town. Sugar Mountain and its hulking ridgetop condo will be visible behind you, as will the distinctive crags of Grandfather Mountain. Up the road from the summit, the labyrinth of private roads through the town of Beech Mountain offers views in all directions.

After surviving the two climbs, it's time for a thrill ride downhill. You'll hurtle through hairpin curves from Beech back to Banner Elk. Smooth N.C. 184 is made for speed. Lean the bike over in the curves, weight the outside pedal hard, and hope the cars won't slow you down.

The descent from Bowers Gap on N.C. 194 is trickier. The road surface poses both physical and mental challenges. You must quickly read the road, decide your line, and make your bike obey. The thick forest is a sun-dappled blur, occasionally opening to wide views of the valley below. When N.C. 194 finally flattens out along Dutch Creek, you can relax and enjoy a mile of easy cruising back to Valle Crucis.

DIRECTIONS TO THE START

From Boone, take N.C. 105 to Broadstone Road (S.R. 1112); the intersection has a traffic signal and a prominent Valle Crucis sign. Turn right on Broadstone Road and proceed 2.7 miles. Turn right onto the gravel access road near the parking lot for the Candy Barrel. A small sign at the head of the drive identifies the area as Valle Crucis Community Park. Leave your vehicle in the parking lot at the park.

DISTANCE

22.4 miles

CHALLENGE

✹✹✹ What this ride lacks in distance it makes up for in altitude gain.

ROAD CONDITIONS AND CAUTIONS

N.C. 194 is a curvy, lightly traveled rural road with limited

Are we there yet? Bold Beech Mountain rises above N.C. 184.

sight distance. N.C. 184 between Banner Elk and Beech Mountain is wider and in better condition, though it is busier. The pockmarked pavement and tight turns on the descent from Bowers Gap to Valle Crucis require caution.

Cues

| 0.0 | Turn **right** out of the dirt driveway from Valle Crucis Community Park onto Broadstone Road (S.R. 1112). |
| 0.1 | Turn **left** just past a small bridge onto N.C. 194 South. |

5.5 You'll reach Bowers Gap at the Avery County line, elevation 4,135 feet. This is the top of the Valle Crucis climb.

7.6 Go **straight** at the traffic signal in Banner Elk.

8.0 Turn **right** onto N.C. 184.

11.2 **Turn around** at the Beech Mountain Town Hall, the finish line for the Tour DuPont stages. The elevation here is 5,085 feet.

14.4 Turn **left** at the stop sign onto N.C. 194 North.

14.8 Go **straight** at the traffic signal in Banner Elk.

16.9 You'll reach Bowers Gap at the Watauga County line, elevation 4,135 feet. Caution: A tricky descent begins here.

22.3 Turn **right** at the stop sign onto Broadstone Road.

22.4 Turn **left** into the driveway at Valle Crucis Community Park.

HIGHEST ELEVATION

5,085 feet near the Beech Mountain Town Hall, 11.2 miles into the ride

Elevation Profile

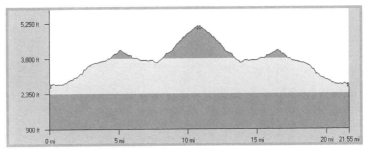

© 2002 DeLorme (www.delorme.com) *Topo USA* ® 4.0

LOWEST ELEVATION

2,670 feet at the start and finish in Valle Crucis

FOOD SERVICES

Restrooms are available seasonally at Valle Crucis Community Park. Stores and restaurants are located in Banner Elk, Beech Mountain, and Valle Crucis. Fred's General Mercantile, just past the turnaround point in Beech Mountain, is a great place to grab a drink and a snack. Fred's motto is, "If we don't have it, you don't need it."

OUTDOOR OPTIONS

The Ski Beech resort offers mountain biking, hiking, golf, and tennis during the warm months. For information, call 800-438-2093 or visit www.SkiBeech.com.

Shull's Mill Road

THE BOONE
BACK ROADS LOOP

SHORT TAKE

You'll get out of town fast on this 24-mile loop ride that begins and ends in downtown Boone, North Carolina. Challenging climbs, swooping descents, level valley riding, and expansive ridge-top views are all just a few short miles from the heart of town. You can ride the loop for a quick workout or use it to hook up with other routes to create truly epic rides. While it's not traffic-free, this route is an alternative to busy U.S. 221/U.S. 321 between Boone and Blowing Rock.

IN DEPTH

Boone has many of the ingredients of a great cycling town.

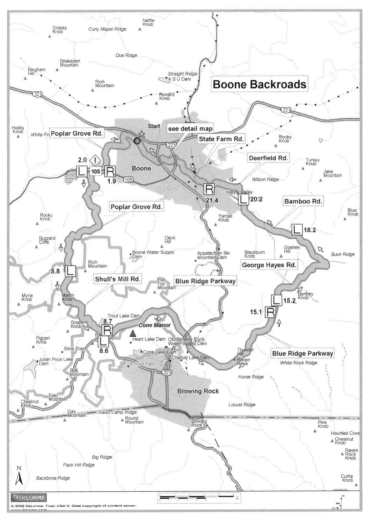

Boone Backroads

Start

see detail map

State Farm Rd.

Poplar Grove Rd.

Deerfield Rd.

2.0

L 105 R
1.9

Boone

Wilson Ridge

Happy Valley

R 21.4

L 20.2

Bamboo Rd.

Poplar Grove Rd.

L 18.2

Boone Water Supply Dam

Appalachian Ski Mountain Dam

George Hayes Rd.

5.8 L

Shull's Mill Rd.

Blue Ridge Parkway

L 15.2

15.1 R

Trout Lake Dam

8.7 R
L
8.6

Cone Manor

Heart Lake Dam

Old Blowing Rock Water Supply Dam

Cone Lake Dam

Chetola Lake Dam

Blue Ridge Parkway

White Rock Ridge

Brown Hill Park

Blowing Rock

N

© DeLORME
© 2002 DeLorme. Topo USA ®. Data copyright of content owner.
www.delorme.com

© 2002 DeLorme (www.delorme.com) *Topo USA* ® 4.0

It's home to a diverse group of cycling enthusiasts, from fit, fast road racers to gonzo mountain bikers. Boone boasts several bike shops to keep riders equipped and a wealth of restaurants and pubs to keep them refreshed. The 12,000 students at Appalachian State University pump youthful energy into the cycling scene. No wonder Lance Armstrong chose Boone as the site for the training camp that helped him bounce back from cancer.

There's just one problem with Boone as a road-cycling destination: traffic. The main routes out of town are all busy and unaccommodating to bikes. Fortunately, the Blue Ridge Parkway and some winding secondary roads offer less-traveled alternatives to the nerve-jangling highways of the High Country.

This great escape begins on Poplar Grove Road, which snakes up a forested hillside above downtown Boone, quickly rising above the noise and traffic of the valley. After a quick jog across busy N.C. 105, Poplar Grove winds into the countryside, revealing the changing face of Watauga County. Hardwood forests, Fraser fir farms, and picturesque Poplar Grove Baptist Church are cheek and jowl with mobile homes, artists' studios, and upscale gated communities.

A twisty descent on Poplar Grove Road ends abruptly at a stop sign, where the ride enters Shull's Mill Road, a former stagecoach route and toll road that's become a cut-through between N.C. 105 and Blowing Rock. The rutted road hugs the side of the mountain, winding through a mature hardwood forest that occasionally opens to views of Grandfather, Hawksbill, and other distinctive peaks.

On one ride up Shull's Mill Road, I saw a puzzling sight. About eight miles into the loop, I spotted two old men sitting on folding chairs on the side of the road, their backs to traffic,

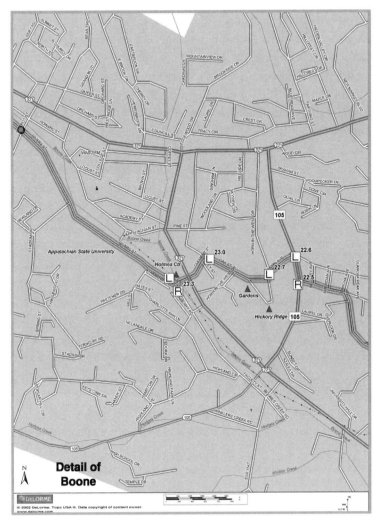

Detail of Boone

N

© 2002 DeLorme (www.delorme.com) *Topo USA* ® 4.0

looking for all the world like they were fishing in the ditch. It turns out they were filling plastic jugs with water tumbling from a metal pipe protruding from the bank. The cool, pure spring water is welcome, as there are no stores or public water sources directly on the route until the finish in Boone.

You'll pick up the Blue Ridge Parkway near Flat Top Manor, a regional crafts outlet and information center located on the former estate of Moses Cone. The descent from the estate to U.S. 221/U.S. 321 is exhilarating. There are no hairpin curves or potholes here. Just hunker down and enjoy the fast, smooth ride.

Past the busy interchange with U.S. 221/U.S. 321, the parkway climbs to the top of a ridge more than 3,800 feet above sea level and 2,500 feet above the Yadkin River Valley. On a clear day, you can see for miles. "A spectacle like ocean waves in a storm" was the way Moravian bishop August Spangenberg described such a view after climbing the ridge at a spot not far from here in 1752. Little has changed since. You're riding along the Eastern Continental Divide, literally atop the Blue Ridge escarpment. Rain on the right of you rolls toward the Atlantic, rain on the left toward the Gulf of Mexico.

The route leaves the parkway at Aho Gap for George Hayes Road. This recently improved rural road serves up one of the finest descents in the High Country. You'll plunge through curve after curve on a wide, smooth road that is sure to satisfy your need for speed. The thrill ride comes to a screeching halt at the stop sign at Bamboo Road. The route then follows Goshen Creek through a flat, peaceful valley that's just a few miles from the hubbub of Boone.

Eventually, it's back to civilization, as the route passes

Appalachian State University's Holmes Convocation Center

Boone's airport and golf course. It intersects the Boone Greenway at Furman Street, which makes for an easy link to the motels, shopping, and restaurants on U.S. 221/U.S. 321. After a short leg on N.C. 105, the route climbs to a pleasant park in the center of town. This park is home to the Daniel Boone Native Gardens, the Hickory Ridge Homestead, and, during the summer months, the outdoor drama *Horn in the West*. The route circles the Holmes Convocation Center and concludes with a cruise down Rivers Street through the campus of Appalachian State University.

This ride can be used as the escape route for longer adventures out of Boone. A right onto Shull's Mill Road from Poplar Grove will point you toward Broadstone Road, the link to Valle Crucis, Beech Mountain, and Cove Creek. A left on Shull's Mill will take you to U.S. 221 and the Blue Ridge Parkway. Follow U.S. 221 northward and you're almost to Blowing Rock. Or take it south to enjoy the Yonahlossee Trail to Grandfather Mountain and Linville. If you pick up the Blue Ridge Parkway going south, you'll be headed toward Julian Price Memorial Park and the Linn Cove Viaduct.

DIRECTIONS TO THE START

Follow U.S. 321/U.S. 421 North (King Street) in downtown Boone. Turn right onto Depot Street. A municipal parking lot is located near the corner of King and Depot Streets. Free parking is available on weekends only in the Appalachian State University parking lot near the corner of Depot and Rivers Streets. The ride begins near the intersection of Depot and Rivers.

DISTANCE

24 miles

CHALLENGE

⊗⊗ The first half of the ride has several short, steep climbs.

ROAD CONDITIONS AND CAUTIONS

This ride is designed to avoid congested routes wherever possible, but traffic is still a concern. Use caution on the short stretches of N.C. 105. The six-mile segment on the Blue Ridge Parkway can be busy on summer weekends and during leaf season. Parkway regulations require cyclists to ride single file.

CUES

0.0   Ride downhill from downtown to the intersection of Depot and Rivers Streets. Turn **right** onto Rivers Street/ Poplar Grove Road.

1.9   Turn **right** at the stop sign onto N.C. 105. Caution: Anticipate heavy traffic here.

2.0   Make a **quick left** onto Poplar Grove Road (S.R. 1552).

5.8   Turn **left** at the stop sign onto Shull's Mill Road (S.R. 1552).

8.6   Turn **left** at the stop sign onto S.R. 1571, a short connecting road to the Blue Ridge Parkway.

8.7   Turn **right** at the stop sign onto the Blue Ridge Parkway and head north.

15.1   Turn **right** onto Sampson Road at Aho, just before the Aho Gap sign. This road is not well marked.

15.2   Make a **quick left** onto George Hayes Road (S.R.1514).

18.2   Turn **left** at the stop sign onto Bamboo Road (S.R. 1524).

20.2   Turn **left** at the stop sign onto Deerfield Road (S.R. 1523).

20.5   Bear **left** to stay on Deerfield Road (now S.R. 1522).

21.4   Turn **right** onto State Farm Road at the Watauga Medical Center.

22.5   Turn **right** onto N.C. 105 at the traffic signal.

22.6   Turn **left** onto Horn Avenue.

22.7   Turn **left** at the stop sign onto Oak Street.

23.0   Turn **left** onto Clement Street.

23.1   Go **straight** across U.S. 321 at the traffic signal.

23.3   Turn **right** at the stop sign at the corner where the Holmes Convocation Center is located, then **left** at the next stop sign onto Rivers Street.

24.0   Make your return to Depot and Rivers Streets.

Elevation Profile

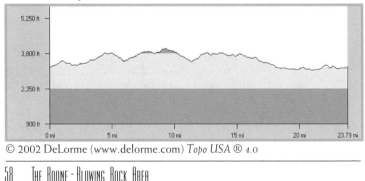

© 2002 DeLorme (www.delorme.com) *Topo USA ® 4.0*

HIGHEST ELEVATION

3,995 feet near the Moses Cone Estate, 9.7 miles into the ride

LOWEST ELEVATION

3,105 feet near the intersection of Deerfield and State Farm Roads, 21.5 miles into the ride

FOOD AND SERVICES

A spring is located on the left side of Shull's Mill Road about 7.9 miles into the ride. Public restrooms and water are available at the Moses Cone Estate, just off the parkway at Milepost 294, some 9.7 miles into the ride. Boone offers a wide range of restaurants and nightspots.

ROADSIDE ATTRACTIONS

Seasonal crafts demonstrations are scheduled daily at the Parkway Craft Center, a Southern Highlands Handicraft Guild shop in Flat Top Manor, the former home of Moses and Bertha Cone. Flat Top Manor is part of the Moses Cone Estate, located off the Blue Ridge Parkway at Milepost 294. For more information, call 828-295-7938.

Outdoor Options

Daniel Boone Native Gardens displays a variety of native plants in a natural setting on its six-acre grounds. An admission fee is charged. Hickory Ridge Homestead, a museum of early mountain life and culture, is nearby. For more information, call 828-264-6390.

Trout Lake, Bass Lake, and the Moses Cone Estate are laced with more than 20 miles of hiking and equestrian trails. Bicycles are not allowed on any parkway trails.

Quiet churchyard along Cove Creek

THE COVE CREEK CRUISE

SHORT TAKE

On this ride, you'll ramble along rushing Cove Creek through a pastoral patch of rural Watauga County once frequented by Daniel Boone. The climb is gradual and the traffic is light, making this cruise ideal for beginners and families who want to try a route that's not pancake-flat. The out-and-back configuration means the ride can be trimmed to virtually any length. After the turnaround, it's a fast cruise down the valley to the finish.

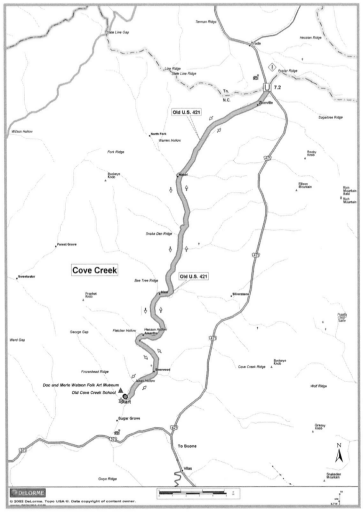

Cove Creek

Old U.S. 421

Old U.S. 421

© 2002 DeLorme (www.delorme.com) *Topo USA* ® 4.0

In Depth

This route traces Cove Creek, a fast-flowing trout stream, almost to its source. As the ride heads up the valley, the creek is a constant presence. You'll cross it one minute, ride alongside it the next, then see it off across a broad field. The creek may disappear behind a church or a thick stand of wildflowers, but eventually you'll see it or hear it again. As the ride steepens, the creek dwindles. Toward the top, you could easily hop across it. The ride reaches its crest at the North Carolina-Tennessee line, which is the turnaround point.

The Cove Creek Valley is rich in history. Daniel Boone headed up the creek on his route over the mountains into Kentucky. The area is rimmed by formidable hills, but the valley itself is long and wide, which invited human settlement. You'll ride through at least five named communities in seven miles, encountering old churches, farmsteads, and the old Cove Creek School, a WPA project listed on the National Register of Historic Places. The former school certainly makes a statement about tradition and change in the mountains; it's home to both the Doc and Merle Watson Folk Art Museum and the Jung Tao School of Classical Chinese Medicine.

The area is still quite rural and has an old-fashioned feel. Hayfields and large plots of burley tobacco occupy the rich bottom land. There are barns aplenty, including several that seem to be on the brink of collapse.

The ride through the valley from the old Cove Creek School to Zionville is uphill, but not oppressively so. The gentle grade has few steep hills. This was once the main highway from Boone to Bristol, Tennessee, but an improved road bypassed Cove

Creek years ago, leaving this route to tractors, not tractor-trailers. The forgiving terrain and low traffic make this a great route for casual riders, families, and folks wanting to attempt that first foray out of flat cycling into the hills.

Of course, what goes up must come down. The ride descends in style with an easy seven-mile whirl back to Sugar Grove. There's no white-knuckle descent here; the downhill is easy to negotiate, with few curves or tricky spots. Ending the ride with a glide puts a positive spin on the whole experience.

DIRECTIONS TO THE START

From Boone, take U.S. 321/U.S. 421 north toward Tennessee. Where the two highways split, bear left on U.S. 321. Turn right at the Cove Creek Store onto Old U.S. 421 (S.R. 1233) in the Sugar Grove community. Go 0.8 mile, turn left on Dale Adams Road, and follow it to the old Cove Creek School. You can leave your car in the parking lot at the school. The ride begins at the intersection of Dale Adams Road and Old U.S. 421.

DISTANCE

14.4 miles

CHALLENGE

⊛ The gentle grade on Old U.S. 421 makes this a ride casual cyclists can enjoy.

Historic Cove Creek School

ROAD CONDITIONS AND CAUTIONS

Old U.S. 421 is lightly traveled. The road surface is grainy and a little bumpy in spots.

CUES

0.0   Turn **left** at the stop sign out of the old Cove Creek School parking lot onto Old U.S. 421 (S.R. 1233).

7.2   **Turn around** at the intersection with U.S. 421.

14.4   Turn **right** onto Dale Adams Road to return to Cove Creek School.

Elevation Profile

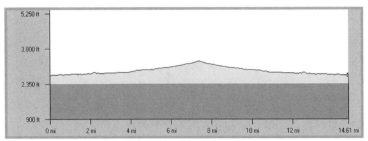

© 2002 DeLorme (www.delorme.com) *Topo USA ®* 4.0

HIGHEST ELEVATION

3,288 feet at U.S. 421 near the Tennessee border, at the halfway point of the ride

LOWEST ELEVATION

2,700 feet crossing Cove Creek in Sugar Grove, near the start and finish

FOOD AND SERVICES

You'll find no food or services directly on the route. The Cove Creek Store is on U.S. 321 less than a mile from the start and finish. Two restaurants and a store are located on U.S. 421 just past the turnaround point. To reach these facilities, turn left on U.S. 421 at the stop sign and enter Tennessee. The store and restaurants are on the left.

ROADSIDE ATTRACTIONS

The Doc and Merle Watson Folk Art Museum, housed in the historic Cove Creek School, hosts the Doc Watson Music Fest each July. For more information, call 828-297-2200 or visit www.covecreek.net.

OUTDOOR OPTIONS

Cove Creek is a stocked trout stream.

Pisa has nothing on Watauga County.

Cresting Mast Gap

THE BULLDOG'S BITE LOOP

SHORT TAKE

You'll flee to the fringes of the High Country on this hilly 32-mile ride. Spectacular scenery, grinding climbs, twisting descents, and, yes, a few crazed canines can be found on this mountainous route through a quiet corner of North Carolina and Tennessee.

IN DEPTH

Warning: The hills on this ride may be haunted.

Local legend has it that a traveler and his dog were killed and then buried beneath Cove Creek School. Folks say a headless ghost dog roams the mountains above the school, looking

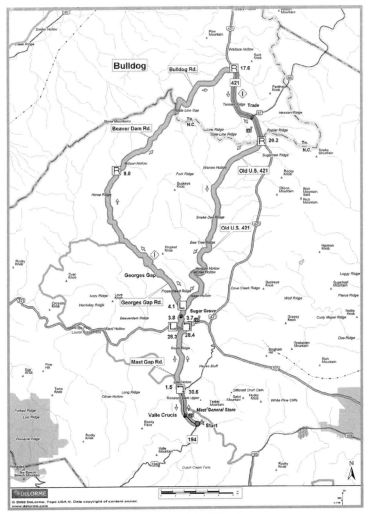

© 2002 DeLorme (www.delorme.com) *Topo USA* ® 4.0

to avenge the murder of his master. So if a menacing, mountain-mean mongrel chases you on this ride, look out. It may not have a head!

The ride will provide you plenty of thrills, even if you don't encounter the haunted hound. It features four descents, including a fast, twisty two-mile plunge from Georges Gap. You'll carve the tight hairpin curves and enjoy the gravity-induced rush.

The ride begins with an easy roll out of Valle Crucis, North Carolina, through the scenic Watauga River Valley. You'll pass Mast General Store, a Valle Crucis mainstay since 1882. The store, which also serves as a post office and community gathering place, reputedly carries everything from cradles to caskets.

Mast Gap Road offers the first climb of the day, a short, steep pull followed by a speedy, straightforward descent to the small community of Sugar Grove. Be sure to enjoy the few miles of flat cycling here, because your heart will be revving to the redline soon enough.

The climb from Cove Creek to the top of unmarked Georges Gap (elevation 3,434 feet) is splendid pain. The road undulates through switchback after switchback, each one lifting you higher and higher above the valley. The road is flanked by high mountain meadows and a succession of old barns. Between the panoramic views and the challenge of the steep climb, the ride up Georges Gap is breathtaking.

The descent from Georges Gap to Beaver Dam Creek is a blur. The road bottoms out in an isolated mountain valley, where you'll see more cattle and horses than people. Burley tobacco grows in the fertile bottom land along the creek during the summer and is hung to dry in big barns in the fall.

Beaver Dam Road offers classic creek-side climbing and a

"I ain't afraid of no dog!"

wide view of the surrounding mountains from the top at State Line Gap, elevation 3,746 feet. Kick back and have a snack under the apple tree at the gap; you've earned it.

The road's name changes to Bulldog Road at the state line, but don't worry; no dog can catch you on this leg of the ride. It's a swift drop down Bulldog from State Line Gap to U.S. 421.

After a couple of miles on busy U.S. 421 through Trade, Tennessee, it's back to the Tar Heel State for an easy back-road cruise downstream along Cove Creek to Sugar Grove. The miles fly by on the gradual descent through the broad valley. The payoff at the top of the ride's final climb at Mast Gap is a view of Grandfather Mountain in the distance. After that, it's a fast return to the Watauga River Valley.

Directions to the Start

From Boone, take N.C. 105 to Broadstone Road (S.R. 1112);

the intersection has a traffic signal and a prominent Valle Crucis sign. Turn right on Broadstone Road and proceed 2.7 miles. Turn right onto the gravel access road near the parking lot for the Candy Barrel. A small sign at the head of the drive identifies the area as Valle Crucis Community Park. Leave your vehicle in the parking lot at the park.

DISTANCE

32.1 miles

CHALLENGE

⊛⊛The Georges Gap climb is the ride's toughest test.

ROAD CONDITIONS AND CAUTIONS

Most of the route follows lightly traveled secondary roads. It takes two short jogs through "downtown" Sugar Grove on busy U.S. 321. A 2.6-mile segment near Trade, Tennessee, follows busy U.S. 421; the wide, smooth-surfaced highway gives passing vehicles room to get by. The twisting two-mile descent from Georges Gap to the Beaver Dam community is very steep and has a succession of tight turns.

CUES

0.0   Turn **right** out of the dirt driveway from Valle Crucis Community Park onto Broadstone Road (S.R. 1112).

0.1	Go **straight** onto N.C. 194 North.
1.5	Turn **left** onto Mast Gap Road (S.R. 1117).
3.7	Turn **left** at the stop sign onto U.S. 321 North.
3.8	Make a **quick right** onto Old U.S. 421 (S.R. 1233).
4.1	Turn **left** onto Georges Gap Road (S.R. 1213).
6.9	You'll reach Georges Gap, elevation 3,434 feet. A steep descent begins here.
9.0	Turn **right** at the old store onto Beaver Dam Road (S.R. 1221).
11.7	Go **straight** at Beaver Dam Baptist Church onto S.R. 1225 (Beaver Dam Road).
14.6	You'll reach State Line Gap (elevation 3,746 feet), where Bulldog Road begins.
17.6	Turn **right** at the stop sign onto U.S. 421 South.
20.2	Turn **right** onto Old U.S. 421 (S.R. 1233) at the state line.
28.3	Turn **left** at the stop sign onto U.S. 321 South.
28.4	Turn **right** onto Mast Gap Road (S.R. 1233).

30.6   Turn **right** at the stop sign onto N.C. 194 South.

32.1   Turn **left** into the driveway to Valle Crucis Community Park.

HIGHEST ELEVATION
3,746 feet at State Line Gap, 14.6 miles into the ride

LOWEST ELEVATION
2,670 feet at the start and finish in Valle Crucis

FOOD AND SERVICES
Restrooms are available seasonally at Valle Crucis Community Park. Stores are located in the North Carolina communities of Sugar Grove and Valle Crucis, as well as in Trade, Tennessee. You'll find two cafés near the North Carolina-Tennessee

Elevation Profile

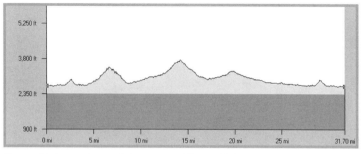

© 2002 DeLorme (www.delorme.com) *Topo USA* ® 4.0

line on U.S. 421 in Trade. Valle Crucis offers a variety of dining options, from sandwiches and ice-cream cones to gourmet fare.

ROADSIDE ATTRACTIONS

Established in 1883, Mast General Store is listed on the National Register of Historic Places. Clothing, outdoor gear, housewares, and general merchandise are sold in the store, which also houses the community's post office. The store is located on N.C. 194 in Valle Crucis. For more information, call 828-963-6511 or visit www.mastgeneralstore.com.

State Line Gap

The century-old Methodist church at Sutherland keeps watch over the valley.

THE TRADE TOUR

SHORT TAKE

This 44-mile out-and-back route rolls through two scenic valleys and dips briefly into the state of Tennessee. The rolling terrain is interrupted by just a few steep hills, making this ride perfect for pacelining. It is rimmed by some of the tallest peaks in the Blue Ridge as it runs through a sparsely populated corner of northwestern North Carolina.

IN DEPTH

This tour meanders through two long valleys that offer miles of rolling terrain.

You'll ride up the Cove Creek Valley first, a gradual pull that ends at the North Carolina-Tennessee line. Daniel Boone trekked through here on his way to Kentucky more than two centuries ago. Today, Cove Creek is flanked by homes, hayfields,

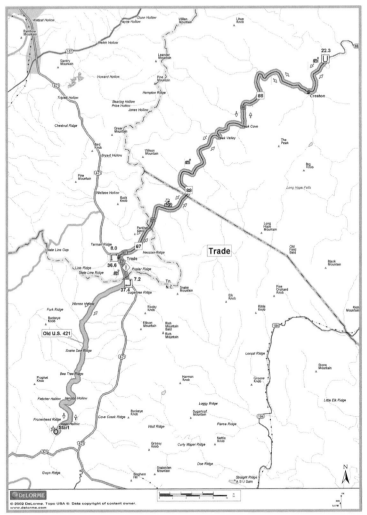

and large plots of tobacco. The peaceful surroundings and relatively flat terrain make the valley a great place to ride.

At the Tennessee line, you'll enter U.S. 421, a well-traveled route between Boone and Bristol. The tour follows U.S. 421 for less than a mile. Decent shoulders and, on the return, a passing lane make this short stretch of highway tolerable for cyclists.

The ride enters tiny Trade, Tennessee, as it descends from the state line on U.S. 421. Two hundred years ago, Trade was a staging ground for pioneers headed west. An old buffalo trail and three wilderness paths converged here, making this a popular trading ground for Native Americans, frontiersmen, and settlers. Today, most of the trading that goes on in Trade is at impromptu flea markets on the side of the road and at the antiques and junk store at the intersection of U.S. 421 and Tenn. 67. Trade's population swells during the last weekend in June, when the annual Trade Days festival showcases Native American and pioneer culture.

The ride turns onto Tenn. 67 to head back toward North Carolina. The climb here is steeper and shorter than the ascent up Cove Creek.

It's not marked in any way, but the crest of the road at the North Carolina-Tennessee line is the division between two of eastern America's great river systems. You've been riding through areas that eventually drain into the Tennessee River. From the state line on, you'll be riding alongside the North Fork of the New River, which flows north to eventually empty into the Ohio.

At the state line, Tenn. 67 becomes N.C. 88, which descends for a few miles into the valley at Sutherland. As you fly down the curvy descent, you can't miss the prominent spire of the century-old Methodist church tucked into the hills at Sutherland.

From Sutherland to Creston, this ride's a glide. You'll pass along the North Fork of the New, which at this point near its headwaters is no more than a glorified creek. Still, this modest stream has carved out a verdant valley beneath some impressive mountains. The first large, conical mountain off to the right past Sutherland is aptly named The Peak. Near Creston, the massive mountain with three distinct bumps on top is Three Top.

The valley here is far from any towns, so it's sparsely populated. The smooth-surfaced, lightly traveled road and fairly flat terrain make this a perfect place to hook up in a paceline and make the miles fly by.

A country store near Creston is the arbitrary turnaround point for the ride. You might continue toward Warrensville and West Jefferson, but bear in mind it will be uphill on N.C. 88 from the turnaround point back to the state line. However far you decide to pedal, the ride ends on a sweet note with a seven-mile gradual downhill along Cove Creek into Sugar Grove.

Backcountry barn on N. C. 88

Directions to the Start

From Boone, take U.S. 321/U.S. 421 north toward Tennessee. Where the routes split, go left on U.S. 321. Turn right at the Cove Creek Store onto Old U.S. 421 (S.R. 1233) in the Sugar Grove community, located about eight miles west of Boone. Go 0.8 mile and turn left on Dale Adams Road to reach the old Cove Creek School. Leave your vehicle in the parking lot at the old school. The ride begins at the intersection of Dale Adams Road and Old U.S. 421.

Distance

44.6 miles

Challenge

⊛⊛On this route, valley riding is punctuated by a few steep climbs.

Road Conditions and Cautions

The route follows busy U.S. 421 for a short distance. All the other roads on the tour are lightly traveled. The road surface on Old U.S. 421 is grainy and a little bumpy in spots.

Cues

0.0   Turn **left** out of the old Cove Creek School parking lot onto Old U.S. 421 (S.R. 1233).

7.2	Turn **left** at the stop sign onto U.S. 421.
8.0	Turn **right** onto Tenn. 67 in Trade, Tennessee.
9.6	Tenn. 67 becomes N.C. 88 at the state line. Continue straight.
22.3	**Turn around** at Mock's Grocery at the intersection of N.C. 88 and Big Laurel Road in Creston, North Carolina.
35.0	N.C. 88 becomes Tenn. 67 at the state line. Continue straight.
36.6	Turn **left** onto U.S. 421 South in Trade, Tennessee.
37.4	Turn **right** at the North Carolina line onto Old U.S. 421 (S.R. 1233).
44.6	Turn **right** onto Dale Adams Road to return to the old Cove Creek School.

HIGHEST ELEVATION

3,511 feet at the state border on Tenn. 67/N.C. 88 at 9.6 miles and again at 35.6 miles into the ride

Elevation Profile

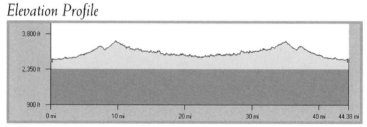

© 2002 DeLorme (www.delorme.com) *Topo USA ® 4.0*

LOWEST ELEVATION

2,700 feet crossing Cove Creek in Sugar Grove near the start and finish

FOOD AND SERVICES

Two restaurants and a store are located on U.S. 421 in Trade, Tennessee. Two stores are on N.C. 88; one is about three miles past the state line and the other is in Creston, North Carolina, at the intersection with Big Laurel Road.

ROAD SIDE ATTRACTIONS

The Doc and Merle Watson Folk Art Museum, housed in the historic Cove Creek School, hosts the Doc Watson Music Fest each July. For more information, call 828-297-2200 or visit www.covecreek.net.

OUTDOOR OPTIONS

Cove Creek and the North Fork of the New River are stocked trout streams.

The West Jefferson Area

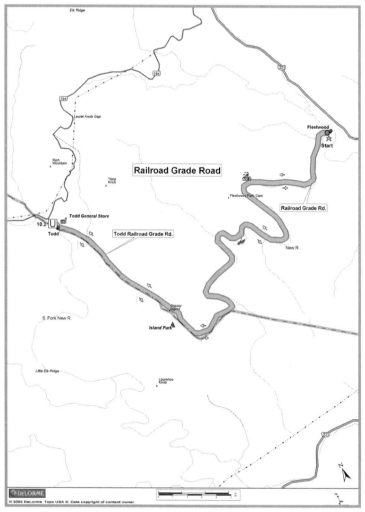

Railroad Grade Road

Todd Railroad Grade Rd.

Todd General Store

Railroad Grade Rd.

Fleetwood

Start

New R.

Island Park

Grassy Island

S. Fork New R.

Little Elk Ridge

Laurence Knob

Elk Ridge

Laurel Knob Gap

Rich Mountain

Third Knob

Fleetwood Falls Dam

Todd

10.2

© 2002 DeLorme (www.delorme.com) *Topo USA* ® 4.0

A serene scene near Todd

A RAMBLE ON RAILROAD GRADE ROAD

SHORT TAKE

The word *easy* doesn't often apply to bike rides in the Blue Ridge High Country, but this 20-mile out-and-back route is just that because it's virtually flat. The level terrain makes it ideal for family riding. This scenic ride rolls along the banks of the South Fork of the New River from the village of Fleetwood, North Carolina, to the slightly less sleepy community of Todd, passing meadows, woodlands, and Christmas-tree farms.

IN DEPTH

Railroad Grade Road got its name for a good reason: It follows the path of an abandoned rail line. Shortly after 1910, hundreds of laborers, mostly Swedes and Italians, began working with

Rolling along the river is fun for all ages.

picks and shovels to create the roadbed that Railroad Grade Road runs along today. The railway from Todd, North Carolina, to Abingdon, Virginia, opened in 1914. It served primarily to haul timber logged from virgin stands of chestnut, oak, and poplar. The line became known as the Virginia Creeper, more an allusion to the train's speed as it lumbered up the steep grade between Damascus, Virginia, and Whitetop Mountain than to the ubiquitous vine of the same name.

The small settlement of Todd isn't a ghost town in the Old West sense, but it's a shell of its former self. Todd burgeoned with the advent of the railroad. The bustling burg boasted two hotels, a variety of stores, a Ford garage, a mill, a pharmacy, several doctors, and a dentist. But what goes boom can also go bust. Todd's crash came during the early days of the Great Depression. The timber petered out, the railroad abandoned the line, local businesses faltered, and the town became just another speck on the map. While the mountains overall have more inhabitants today than ever before, there are plenty of spots that are less populated than they were decades ago, and Todd is one of them.

Today, Todd is tiny, but it's alive and kicking. Constructed in 1914 in anticipation of the railroad, Todd General Store continues to do a good trade, especially with visitors during the summer. Appalachian Outfitters, located in the old train station, rents bikes, kayaks, canoes, and tubes. The citizens of Todd have pitched in to preserve the community's history, partly by building two community parks and staging a successful summer concert series. This ride, some homemade cookies from the general store, and some tunes from one of the free concerts would be a great combination.

The popular bike ride from Fleetwood to Todd attracts families, senior citizens, and even local hammerheads wanting a flat time-trial site. It follows the twisting banks of the South Fork of the New River, a federally recognized American Heritage River. The New is an oddball as rivers go. It flows north, not south. Geologists consider the New to be perhaps the oldest river on the continent, name notwithstanding. Exasperated explorer August Spangenberg said of the New in 1752, "This river runs north, now south, now east, now west, in short to all points of the compass." As my family has pointed out to me many times, this is a ride where you can have a headwind out *and* back.

With no turns and no appreciable gain or loss of elevation, the route couldn't be easier to follow or finish. The scenery is a sampler of the New River Valley. You'll pedal past large, open fields, forests, bluffs, and Christmas-tree farms. The river itself is rarely out of view. It's a clear, shallow, slow-moving stream that teems with activity during the summer. You'll see paddlers, waders, folks fishing for smallmouth bass, and even an occasional baptism (if you ride on a Sunday).

The route can be ridden in either direction, but starting in Fleetwood makes Todd the halfway point. It's a natural place to stop and rest awhile. The ride from Todd to Fleetwood should be a tad bit easier, as it follows the river downstream, but the whims of the mountain winds mean that's not always the case.

DIRECTIONS TO THE START

To begin in Fleetwood, go north on U.S. 221 for 5.5 miles from the U.S. 421 intersection at Deep Gap. Turn left onto Railroad Grade Road (S.R. 1106) just past Fleetwood School. Drive down the hill into the river valley to the post office in Fleetwood. A grass parking lot is located across from the post office.

To begin in Todd, go north on N.C. 194 for 11 miles from Boone. Turn right onto Todd Railroad Grade Road (S.R. 1100) just past the Todd Volunteer Fire Department. Drive down the hill to Walter and Annie Cook Memorial Park, on the right across from Todd General Store. You can leave your vehicle in the parking lot at the park.

DISTANCE

20.4 miles

CHALLENGE

❡ Kids, seniors, and even out-of-shape riders can have fun on this flat route.

Road Conditions and Cautions

The entire route is paved, though it has occasional potholes. The road is narrow—one lane wide in spots. Popular with both bikes and cars on summer weekends, this laid-back route encourages two-abreast riding, but be aware of vehicles approaching from either direction and pull over to allow them to pass.

Cues

0.0   Turn **left** out of the parking area across from the post office in Fleetwood onto Railroad Grade Road (S.R.1106).

10.2   **Turn around** at Todd.

20.4   You'll end the ride at the parking area in Fleetwood.

Riders rule the road on this riverside route.

Elevation Profile

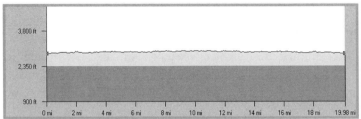

© 2002 DeLorme (www.delorme.com) *Topo USA ® 4.0*

HIGHEST ELEVATION

2,984 feet at Todd, 10.2 miles into the ride

LOWEST ELEVATION

2,859 feet at the start and finish in Fleetwood

FOOD AND SERVICES

No facilities are available at the start of the ride in Fleetwood; a country store is located on U.S. 221 at its intersection with Railroad Grade Road. Todd General Store has sandwiches, homemade baked goods, and an eclectic assortment of candy, drinks, and general merchandise.

ROADSIDE ATTRACTIONS

Joe Morgan, the owner of Todd General Store, isn't running just a commercial establishment here. This venerable store is also a mountain-music hot spot. Acoustic jam sessions are held at the store Friday nights at seven. A summer music series is held Saturday afternoons across the road at Walter and Annie Cook Memorial Park. For more information, call 336-877-1067 or visit http://toddgeneralstore.com.

Outdoor Options

Rental canoes, kayaks, and inner tubes are available at Appalachian Outfitters in Todd. For more information, call 336-877-8800.

The New River's smallmouth bass attract anglers. The portion of the river near the bridge at Castle Ford Road is popular with waders.

Taking a break atop Snake—riders rest at Pottertown Gap.

THE SNAKE MOUNTAIN LOOP

SHORT TAKE

This 42-mile loop traces the steep, coiled route up Snake Mountain, one of the toughest road climbs in the Blue Ridge High Country. The route descends into a deep valley, following the North Fork of the New River downstream. In addition to the Snake Mountain ascent, the ride includes two category-four climbs featured in the Tour DuPont. It begins and ends in historic Todd, North Carolina.

IN DEPTH

Only two species of venomous snakes inhabit the hills: the

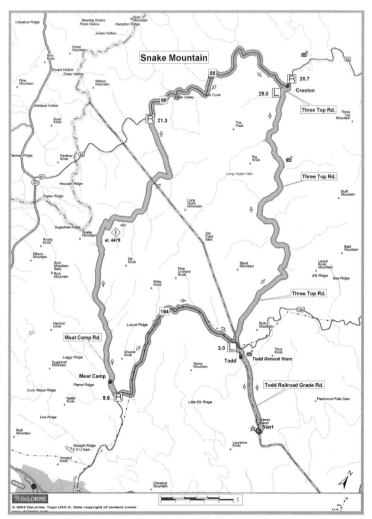

Snake Mountain

88
R 28.7
29.0 L Creston

Three Top Rd.

88
88
R 21.3

Three Top Rd.

i
el. 4479

Three Top Rd.

194
194
3.0 L
Todd
Todd General Store

Meat Camp Rd.

Meat Camp

Todd Railroad Grade Rd.

9.9 R

Start

© 2002 DeLorme (www.delorme.com) *Topo USA* ® 4.0

© 2002 DeLorme, Topo USA ®. Data copyright of content owner.

reclusive, relatively rare timber rattler and the less potent, more commonly encountered copperhead. Most of the snakes in the High Country are actually beneficial. But snakes, venomous or not, aren't esteemed creatures here. Many mountaineers will go after a snake with a hoe or back up the pickup just to run over it twice. Adam and Eve were conned by a snake, a fact many folks in the mountains just can't seem to get past.

So when a bike ride crosses Snake Mountain, you should expect something wicked. This route features three significant climbs, the most remarkable of which is the one up Snake Mountain. The climb technically crosses Pottertown Gap, a high mountain pass at 4,479 feet that separates Watauga County's Snake Mountain and Elk Knob. The ascent begins innocently enough in Meat Camp (elevation 3,180 feet), a community whose roots go back to pioneer days, when bands of hunters from the foothills would follow the old buffalo trail up the mountain in pursuit of game. S.R. 1340 runs along Meat Camp Creek, barely rising for several miles as the road passes open fields and the old Winebarger gristmill. Does this snake have no bite?

Then the climb begins. It's not long, but it is steep—then steeper, then walk-the-bike, cry-to-your-mama steep. A photographer was stationed at the top of this climb during the 2000 Blood, Sweat and Gears ride. I wasn't sure if he was snapping souvenirs or potential obituary shots.

Once atop unmarked Pottertown Gap, it's like a scene out of *The Sound of Music*. Snake Mountain looms large on the left. A mountain meadow overlooks ridge after ridge of hills before you and behind you. It's a great place to stop, catch your breath, and enjoy the hard-earned view.

The descent is longer and more gradual than the climb. The

A paceline pumps up Three Top Road.

few tricky curves toward the top of the mountain soon give way to some straight downhill stretches. The ride turns to follow the North Fork of the New River at Sutherland, elevation 3,080 feet; if you look to the right near the stop sign, you'll see a beautiful, old Methodist church high on the hill.

During the next several miles, you'll enjoy blissful valley cruising down N.C. 88. A large peak—named, not coincidentally, The Peak—looms over the route. The ride snakes along Peak Valley and the North Fork of the New. Peaceful, pastoral, and rimmed by hills, this deep valley is sparsely populated and relatively untouched by development.

The ride leaves the North Fork at Creston, near another historic Methodist church. It follows rushing Three Top Creek, crossing the trout stream over and over. Be thankful for bridges; a traveler on horseback in 1899 wrote that he crossed this creek 31 times in six miles! The bold stream fades to a small branch as the route follows the creek up to its headwaters. This climb and the one up Elk Ridge on N.C. 194 at the start of the ride were tackled by some of the world's best cyclists during stage seven of the 1994 Tour DuPont.

The Three Top climb tops out at a nondescript crest 3,470 feet in elevation. Then it's a long, fast descent back to Todd, where the general store awaits with its cornucopia of goodies for pooped pedalers. After miles of grinding climbs, it feels great to spin the flat three-mile stretch along the New River back to Island Park.

DIRECTIONS TO THE START

From Boone, drive north on N.C. 194 approximately 11 miles to Todd. Just past the Todd Volunteer Fire Department, turn right onto Todd Railroad Grade Road (S.R. 1100). Proceed approximately 3 miles to the parking area near the bridge at Castle Ford Road.

From U.S. 421 South, turn right on Brownwood Road, then left at the stop sign onto Todd Railroad Grade Road. Proceed 1.1 miles to the parking area near the bridge at Castle Ford Road.

You can leave your vehicle in the parking area at Island Park, located near the intersection of Castle Ford Road and Todd Railroad Grade Road. The ride begins at the intersection.

DISTANCE

42.5 miles

CHALLENGE

⊗⊗∉ Snake Mountain is a wall to remember.

Road Conditions and Cautions

The roads on this route are generally lightly traveled. The descent from Pottertown Gap has sharp curves near the top; be on the lookout for gravel in the roadway.

Cues

0.0   Turn **left** at the stop sign from Castle Ford Road onto Todd Railroad Grade Road and head toward Todd.

3.0   Turn **left** at the stop sign onto N.C. 194 South.

9.9   Turn **right** at the Meat Camp Volunteer Fire Department onto Meat Camp Road (S.R. 1340).

15.2   You'll reach Pottertown Gap, elevation 4,479 feet. A steep descent begins here.

21.3   Turn **right** at the stop sign onto N.C. 88 North.

28.7   Turn **right** onto Three Top Road (S.R. 1100).

29.0   Make a **quick left** to remain on Three Top Road.

39.5   Go **straight** at the stop sign at N.C. 194.

42.5   The ride ends at Island Park.

Elevation Profile

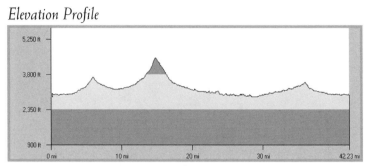

© 2002 DeLorme (www.delorme.com) *Topo USA* ® 4.0

HIGHEST ELEVATION

4,479 feet at the top of the climb to Pottertown Gap, 15.2 miles into the ride

LOWEST ELEVATION

2,864 feet at Creston, 28.7 miles into the ride

FOOD AND SERVICES

Water and restrooms are available at Todd General Store located 3 miles from the start and finish of the ride. A small, nondescript country store is located at the intersection of Three Top Road and Ben Bolen Road (S.R. 1125).

ROADSIDE ATTRACTIONS

Todd General Store, a venerable establishment opened in 1914, is also a mountain-music hot spot. Acoustic jam sessions are held here Friday nights at seven. A summer music series is held Saturday afternoons across from the store at Walter and Annie Cook Memorial Park. For more information, call 336-877-1067 or visit http://toddgeneralstore.com.

OUTDOOR OPTIONS

Meat Camp Creek, Three Top Creek, and the North Fork of the New River are stocked trout streams.

Rental canoes, kayaks, and inner tubes are available at Appalachian Outfitters in Todd. For more information, call 336-877-8800.

Smallmouth bass attract anglers to the South Fork of the New. The portion of the river near the bridge at Castle Ford Road is popular with waders.

A pastoral scene along the North Fork of the New River

Three Top Mountain

THE BUFFALO TRAIL TREK

SHORT TAKE

You can escape the herd on this 37-mile loop through the highlands of Ashe County, North Carolina. You'll trace the tracks of wild buffalo along Buffalo Creek, pass between two of the most ecologically significant peaks in the southern Appalachians, conquer a daunting climb, and soar down several multimile descents on this scenic and challenging route.

IN DEPTH

August Spangenberg was one brave bishop.

In 1752, the Moravian minister left the comforts of Penn-

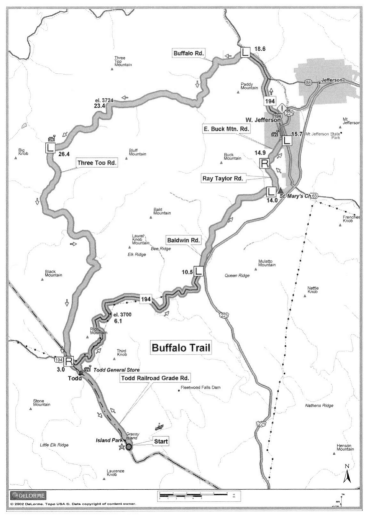

© 2002 DeLorme (www.delorme.com) *Topo USA* ® 4.0

sylvania for the wilds of the Appalachian frontier in search of land where his flock of religious immigrants could worship freely. Before he claimed the Wachovia tract near what is now Winston-Salem, Bishop Spangenberg traversed the rugged terrain of the Blue Ridge High Country just as winter was coming on.

The bishop's party, misled by a disoriented guide, scaled the Blue Ridge near what is now Blowing Rock. The men clambered on hands and knees up the side of the mountain as their horses trembled. Once atop what Spangenberg called "the frightful mountain," the group spent the better part of two weeks navigating a nearly impenetrable maze of hills and valleys through what are now Watauga, Ashe, and Wilkes Counties. They were the first white men ever to visit these high mountains.

Wolves howled and panthers prowled. Snow blew in the whipping wind. "Our men lost heart," a despairing Spangenberg wrote in his diary. "Our horses would die, and we with them." Routes through the rocky ridges and laurel hells were hard to come by. "Why do I speak of a road when there is none but the buffalo have made?" Spangenberg wrote. For centuries, wandering herds of bison had trampled crude paths through the forbidding terrain.

Wild buffalo have long since been extirpated from the High Country, but their trails live on. The same paths blazed by bison and used by Native Americans and pioneers were, as writer Roy Thompson puts it, "eventually approved at great expense by engineers," becoming roadways that are still in use today.

This route begins in the New River Valley not far from one of those legendary buffalo trails. It loops through the high mountains of Ashe County, eventually running along Buffalo Creek through a deep valley where a few bison still roam today, albeit behind sturdy fences. Riders won't experience the fear and bewilderment Spangenberg and his men knew, but they will have to contend with a wicked, wall-like climb on Buffalo Road that is one of the steepest in the High Country.

The ride starts with an easy three-mile warmup along the South Fork of the New River on flat Railroad Grade Road. Spangenberg and his party explored this winding river extensively before turning back down the Blue Ridge.

At Todd, the route leaves the New River Valley to begin a loop of some of the High Country's loftiest peaks. You'll follow N.C. 194, a state-designated Scenic Byway, as it winds northward along the side of Elk Ridge. The 700-foot climb over three miles to unmarked Laurel Knob Gap is followed by a long, smooth, speedy descent off the ridge.

It's an easy cruise as the route follows Beaver Creek downstream toward West Jefferson. Christmas-tree farms cover the broad valley floor. Mount Jefferson rises in the distance; a power-line corridor bisects the large knob's south face, making this landmark easily recognizable.

Cruising along Three Top Road

The route jogs around a busy shopping area on the outskirts of West Jefferson. St. Mary's Episcopal Church, home of several renowned frescoes by artist Ben Long, is just past the turn onto Ray Taylor Road.

A quick plunge on East Buck Mountain Road leads to downtown West Jefferson. You'll pass shops, restaurants, and several large murals on Jefferson Avenue, the main drag through downtown. If you're so inclined, you can see cheese made at the Ashe County Cheese Company, just off the route on East Main Street. You'll then have to grit your teeth for a few miles of tedious riding along busy N.C. 194 out of West Jefferson.

Riding nirvana awaits you as the route departs the highway at Buffalo Road. The ride up the beautiful Buffalo Valley is a delight. Buffalo Road meanders along rushing Buffalo Creek, passing farms and forests. The valley is framed by two towering mountains—Bluff Mountain on the left and jagged Three Top Mountain to the right. The crags of Three Top become more and more prominent as the route gently climbs toward the top of the long valley. These high mountains flanking Buffalo Creek comprise one of the most ecologically diverse areas in the Southeast. The substrate of rare calcium-rich rock nurtures an amazing variety of plants. An unusual wetland at Bluff Mountain harbors 90 rare, threatened, or endangered species. The Nature Conservancy protects more than 4,000 acres at Bluff Mountain and Three Top Mountain.

The climb to the gap separating these two 5,000-foot sentinels is short and painful. Once the road departs the valley floor, it climbs more than 400 feet in just over two-thirds of a mile, for an average grade of 13 percent. This climb, the Heartbreak Hill of the annual Blue Ridge Brutal 100 century ride, has

Bluff Mountain is the backdrop for a short, steep climb.

turned many riders into walkers.

As you catch your breath atop the gap, turn around to appreciate just how high you've climbed. From this high pass, the entire Buffalo Valley is splayed below, flanked by massive ridges on either side.

It's a quick zip down the mountain to Three Top Creek. Three Top Road weaves along the creek through a high mountain valley, following the trout stream as it dwindles to a small branch. The Tour DuPont roared through this sleepy valley in 1994.

A screaming three-mile downhill leads back to Todd. Ravenous riders are sure to find something good to eat in the creaky old Todd General Store. The ride ends with a flat three-mile cool-down along the banks of the New River.

DIRECTIONS TO THE START

From Boone, go north on N.C. 194 for approximately 11 miles to Todd. Just past the Todd Volunteer Fire Department, turn right onto Todd Railroad Grade Road (S.R. 1100). Proceed approximately 3 miles to the parking area near the bridge at Castle Ford Road.

From U.S. 421 South, turn right on Brownwood Road. Turn left at the stop sign onto Todd Railroad Grade Road. Proceed 1.1 miles to the parking area near the bridge at Castle Ford Road.

You can leave your vehicle at the parking area at Island Park, located near the intersection of Castle Ford Road and Todd Railroad Grade Road. The ride begins at the intersection.

DISTANCE

37.1 miles

CHALLENGE

✪ ✪ᕥ The climb from Buffalo Creek is wickedly steep.

ROAD CONDITIONS AND CAUTIONS

Most of the roads on this route are lightly traveled and in good condition. The three-mile stretch of N.C. 194 from downtown West Jefferson to Buffalo Road is busy. Beware of several wheel-sucking storm drains on N.C. 194 just past downtown West Jefferson.

Cues

0.0	Turn **left** at the stop sign from Castle Ford Road onto Todd Railroad Grade Road (S.R. 1100).
3.0	Turn **right** at the stop sign onto N.C. 194 North.
6.1	You'll reach Laurel Knob Gap, elevation 3,705 feet.
10.5	Turn **left** just before U.S. 221 onto Baldwin Road (S.R. 1248).
14.0	Turn **left** onto Ray Taylor Road (S.R. 1133).
14.9	Turn **right** at the stop sign onto East Buck Mountain Road (S.R. 1134).
15.7	Turn **left** at the traffic signal onto Jefferson Avenue (U.S. 221 Business/N.C. 194).
16.2	Continue **straight** to follow N.C. 194.
18.6	Turn **left** onto Buffalo Road (S.R. 1131).
20.6	Go **straight** onto Central Buffalo Road (S.R. 1133).
21.1	Go **straight** onto West Buffalo Road (S.R.1125).

23.4   You'll reach the top of the climb, elevation 3,724 feet, and begin Ben Bolen Road (S.R. 1125).

26.4   Turn **left** at the stop sign onto Three Top Road (S.R. 1100).

34.1   Go **straight** at the stop sign across N.C. 194 onto Todd Railroad Grade Road.

37.1   You'll end the ride at Island Park.

HIGHEST ELEVATION

3,724 feet at the top of the climb on West Buffalo Road, 23.4 miles into the ride

LOWEST ELEVATION

2,782 feet near the intersection of N.C. 194 and Buffalo Road, 15.8 miles into the ride

Elevation Profile

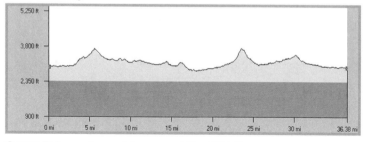

© 2002 DeLorme (www.delorme.com) *Topo USA* ® 4.0

FOOD AND SERVICES

Water and restrooms are available at Todd General Store, located 3 miles from the start and finish. You'll find stores and restaurants in West Jefferson. A small, nondescript country store is located at the intersection of Three Top Road and Ben Bolen Road (S.R. 1125).

ROADSIDE ATTRACTIONS

St. Mary's Episcopal Church, just past Ray Taylor Road on Beaver Creek School Road in West Jefferson, is a simple mountain church that houses numerous pieces of religious art, including three frescoes by Ben Long. For more information, call 336-982-3076.

Monday through Saturday, you can see cheese made at the Ashe County Cheese Company, located at 106 East Main Street in West Jefferson. For more information, call 336-246-2501.

Todd General Store, a venerable establishment opened in 1914, is a mountain-music hot spot. Acoustic jam sessions are held at the store Friday nights at seven. A summer music series is held Saturday afternoons in Walter and Annie Cook Memorial Park across from the store. For more information, call 336-877-1067 or visit http://toddgeneralstore.com.

OUTDOOR OPTIONS

The Nature Conservancy's North Carolina office offers field trips to the Bluff Mountain Preserve. For more information, call 919-403-8558 or visit www.tnc.org/northcarolina.

Three Top Creek is a stocked trout stream.

Rental canoes, kayaks, and inner tubes are available at Appalachian Outfitters in Todd. Call 336-877-8800.

Smallmouth bass attract anglers to the South Fork of the New River. The portion of the river near the bridge at Castle Ford Road is popular with waders.

It's beginning to look a lot like Christmas along N.C. 113.

FOUNTAIN OF YOUTH: THE SHATLEY SPRINGS TOUR

SHORT TAKE

You'll work up a hearty appetite on this 32-mile ride that begins and ends at Shatley Springs, a mountain inn famous for its healing waters and all-you-can-eat country-style meals. The route winds through highlands and valleys along the back roads in North Carolina's Ashe and Alleghany Counties. Highlights include two peaceful stretches along the picturesque New River and a glimpse of Christmas yet to come along N.C. 113.

IN DEPTH

Martin Shatley was ready to kill himself.

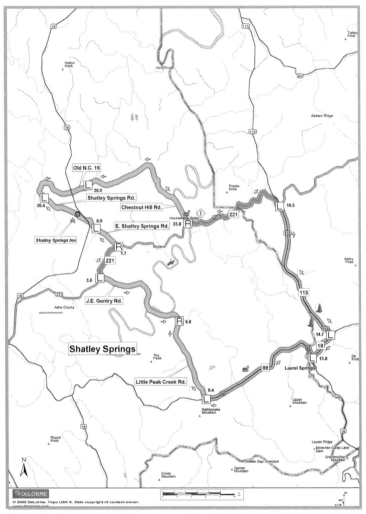

Old N.C. 16

28.0

Shatley Springs Rd.

30.4

Chestnut Hill Rd.

0.9

E. Shatley Springs Rd.

23.6

Shatley Springs Inn

19.5

221

1.7

221

3.0

J.E. Gentry Rd.

113

6.6

Shatley Springs

14.7

18

13.8

88

Laurel Springs

Little Peak Creek Rd.

9.4

DeLorme

© 2002 DeLorme. Topo USA ®. Data copyright of content owner.
www.delorme.com

© 2002 DeLorme (www.delorme.com) *Topo USA* ® 4.0

It was 1890, and Shatley suffered from a long list of afflictions, including indigestion, a bad cough, a bleeding lung, and night sweats. Worst of all, his skin was literally raw. "Many nights I scratched myself all night until my skin bled most all over," Shatley recalled. "I lost all hope of getting well."

On a hot summer day, Shatley paused at an Ashe County spring to splash water on his inflamed face. The chance encounter changed his life. The water bubbling out of Little Phoenix Mountain cured Martin Shatley, and he spread the word like a man possessed. Folks flocked to Shatley's spring seeking cures. An inn, a fishing lake, and cabins sprang up at the site, all to serve tourists drawn by the lure of healing water.

The water from Shatley Springs contains many trace mineral elements, including radium. It's available from a free tap on the south side of the inn. It's a good idea to fill a water bottle or two with the elixir before you head out. It'll put a spring in your pedal stroke for the rolling hills on this loop ride.

There are some long hills along the route, but no wildly canted, switchback-plagued slopes. You'll zoom downhill in full aero tuck on some of these roller-coaster hills and be able to coast nearly to the top of the next rise.

The ride dips into the New River Valley twice. You'll first encounter the South Fork of the New after a fast descent on J. E. Gentry Road. The road twists in time with Silas Branch, following the small stream through open fields and a cool, shady stand of rhododendron. Suddenly, you'll pop out into the sunshine and cross the river. Check out the view of the wide, unspoiled valley from the bridge. This idyllic scene brings to mind the comforting green pastures of the 23rd Psalm. The route picks up the federally recognized American Heritage River again 14 miles later at the New River General Store and Outfitters, an old, two-story frame building stocked with everything from hoop cheese to topographic maps. It then turns onto Chestnut Hill Road, a narrow country lane that follows the New for a mile or so before climbing into the surrounding hills.

Between the two valley sojourns, the ride rolls along some sparsely traveled highways featuring old farms, big views, and Christmas trees by the thousands. North Carolina produces about 4 million live Christmas trees a year, nearly all of them grown in the Blue Ridge High Country. It's Christmas as far as the eye can see as you turn onto N.C. 113 north of Laurel Springs. Huge stands of Fraser firs line both sides of the road from the valley floor to the tops of the surrounding hills. You're pedaling past future Christmases for thousands of American families. It takes 12 years and about 100 visits from the grower for these trees to mature from seedlings to seven-footers.

There are plenty of interesting sights on this route, but the ride might be most memorable for its smells: tangy burley tobacco curing in big barns in the fall; pine sawdust piled high at the sawmill; the damp, woodsy smell along the creek before it spills into the New River; and the intoxicating aroma of Shatley Springs Inn at the end of the ride. Only the most dedicated dieter could ignore the seductive scent of fried chicken, country ham, buttermilk biscuits, vegetables, and homemade desserts.

By the time you pedal back into the Shatley Springs parking lot at the end of this 32-mile ride, you will have cranked nearly 10,000 pedal strokes, burning up well over 1,000 calories along the way. Forget the water; it's time to eat!

*New River
General Store*

DIRECTIONS TO THE START

From Jefferson, take N.C. 16 about six miles north. Turn
left onto Shatley Springs Road (S.R. 1574). The entrance to
Shatley Springs Inn is on the left just down the hill. The ride
leaves from the parking area at the inn. Always ask for permission before parking in any private lot.

DISTANCE

32 miles

CHALLENGE

⊗⊗ Hills, yes. Supersteep, multimile climbs, no.

ROAD CONDITIONS AND CAUTIONS

The roads on the route are lightly to moderately traveled.
U.S. 221 from the Ashe County line to the New River bridge is
poorly surfaced, making the descent into the valley a bit tricky.

"He leadeth me beside the still waters."

CUES

0.0   Turn **right** out of the Shatley Springs Inn parking lot onto Shatley Springs Road (S.R. 1574).

0.3   Turn **left** at the stop sign onto N.C. 16 North.

0.4   Make a **quick right** onto East Shatley Springs Road (S.R. 1571).

0.9   Turn **left** at the stop sign and continue on East Shatley Springs Road.

1.7   Turn **right** at the stop sign onto U.S. 221 South.

3.0   Turn **left** just past the top of the hill onto J. E. Gentry Road (S.R. 1593).

5.3   Go **straight** at the New River bridge.

6.6   Turn **right** onto Little Peak Creek Road (S.R. 1595); note that the green sign at the intersection lists it as S.R. 1522.

9.4   Turn **left** at the stop sign onto N.C. 88 East.

13.8   Turn **left** at the fork, then **left** at the stop sign onto N.C. 18 North, heading toward Sparta.

14.7   Turn **left** at the bottom of the hill onto N.C. 113 North.

19.5   Turn **left** at the flashing light at the bottom of the hill onto U.S. 221 South.

23.6   Turn **right** just past the New River bridge onto Chestnut Hill Road (S.R. 1567).

28.0   Turn **left** at the stop sign onto Old N.C. 16 (S.R. 1573).

28.9   Go **straight** under the N.C. 16 overpass.

30.4   Turn **left** onto Shatley Springs Road.

32.0   Turn **right** into the driveway at Shatley Springs Inn to end the ride.

Elevation Profile

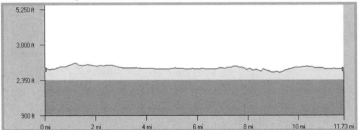

© 2002 DeLorme (www.delorme.com) *Topo USA ®* 4.0

HIGHEST ELEVATION

3,172 feet on N.C. 113, approximately 16 miles into the ride

LOWEST ELEVATION

2,548 feet along the New River on Chestnut Hill Road, 23.6 miles into the ride

FOOD AND SERVICES

Restrooms, food, and water are available at Shatley Springs Inn. There is a country store on N.C. 88 about 10 miles into the ride. The New River General Store is located at the intersection of U.S. 221 and Chestnut Hill Road, 23.6 miles into the ride.

ROADSIDE ATTRACTIONS

The New River General Store, on U.S. 221 at Chestnut

Hill Road, is the oldest continuously operating general store in the area. Old-fashioned candies, hoop cheese, local crafts, and supplies are sold here. For more information, call 336-982-9192.

Shatley Springs Inn, on N.C. 16 north of Jefferson, serves family-style, home-cooked meals seven days a week. It is open seasonally. According to *Our State* magazine, the inn serves the "Best Breakfast in North Carolina." The water here reputedly has healing powers; it's free from a tap on the side of the inn. Reservations are recommended. For more information, call 336-982-2236 or visit www.shatleysprings.com.

OUTDOOR OPTIONS

New River Outfitters, located at U.S. 221 and Chestnut Hill Road, rents canoes and inner tubes. For more information, call 800-982-9190 or visit www.canoethenew.com.

Low water bridge over the New River near Glendale Springs

THE TOUR DE FRESCOES

SHORT TAKE

This 23-mile loop links two Ashe County churches that house renowned works of religious art. Short, steep climbs, mountain vistas, and the splendor of the New River are also attractions on this ride, which begins and ends on the Blue Ridge Parkway near the village of Glendale Springs.

IN DEPTH

The concept of the religious pilgrimage, while out of fashion in the Western world, runs deep in the world's great

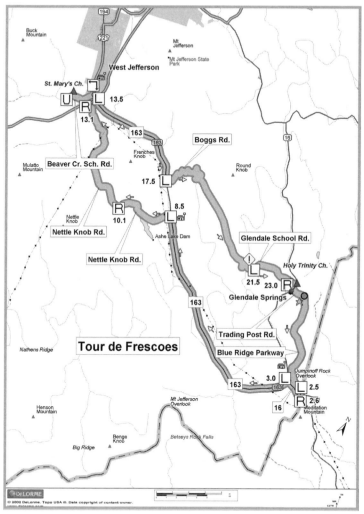

Tour de Frescoes

St. Mary's Church

religions. All able-bodied Muslims are required by the Koran to complete a pilgrimage, or Hajj, to Mecca. Jews and Christians, too, have for centuries visited venerated sites in the Holy Land in quest of spiritual renewal. These disparate faiths seems to agree that there's something to be gained in undertaking an arduous journey to a holy place.

Jefferson's not Jerusalem, but two century-old Episcopal churches in Ashe County attract upwards of 50,000 pilgrims a year. They are drawn by striking frescoes of Christian themes, housed in small, simple mountain churches. The frescoes are the work of North Carolina artist Ben Long, who went to Italy in the early 1970s and studied the ancient art of applying mineral pigments to freshly laid plaster.

The ride starts at the Northwest Trading Post in Glendale Springs, a regional crafts shop less than a half-mile from Holy Trinity Episcopal Church. You could walk to see *The Last Supper* from the trading post. Instead, the route takes off toward Beaver Creek, heading toward St. Mary's, the other, less widely known "Church of the Frescoes."

The ride passes through pastureland, then descends into the New River Valley for a few flat miles. An ancient cemetery near the bridge over the New River has a fence-post-shaped gravestone with the initials *TC* carved on it. Local legend has it that Daniel Boone shot a deer here, and that the deer fell on the stone. Boone supposedly carved the *TC* in honor of his friend and hunting companion Colonel Tom Calloway, making yet another mark on the High Country.

The arduous part of this pilgrimage begins about eight miles in, when the route departs rolling N.C. 163 for the steeper hills of Nettle Knob Road. The payoff is a panoramic view from the top of the ridge before a hasty descent to a busy shopping area on the outskirts of West Jefferson.

You'll run a short gauntlet of convenience stores and fast-food joints before you arrive at St. Mary's, a modest white frame church. Go inside; the dress code is casual enough to allow Lycra. Three Ben Long frescoes are displayed here. Two small works—*Mary, Great With Child* and *John the Baptist*—flank the altar. A third fresco, *The Mystery of Faith,* is a graphic depiction of the crucified Christ juxtaposed with an ethereal image of the risen Lord. It covers the entire back wall of the church and towers over a simple altar.

The ride cruises out of West Jefferson on N.C. 163, then veers left onto Boggs Road. A short, steep climb soon gives way to a twisty descent to the New River. You'll pass the Elk Shoals Campground, a mecca for generations of Methodists. The river is wide, flat, and shallow—perfect for wading on a hot summer day. In July 1998, President Clinton declared the New an American Heritage River from a spot not far from here.

You'll cross the river on a wooden, one-lane, low-water

bridge. The route follows a dirt road for about a quarter-mile, a distance short enough for hoofing it, if you don't want to risk a flat.

It then turns left onto Glendale School Road for a climb out of the valley to Holy Trinity Episcopal Church. It passes through large, open fields that are covered with Queen Anne's lace in the summer. The church is at the top of the hill in the quaint village of Glendale Springs.

Holy Trinity houses Ben Long's depiction of the Last Supper, a work renowned for its depth and realism. Local folk served as models for the disciples depicted around the table. The fresco's design is integrated with the beams of the church, creating a three-dimensional effect. The church was officially closed in 1946 and not used again until 1980, when Long and his assistants finished the fresco. *The Last Supper* revived not only the church, but also the sleepy community around it. Today, Glendale Springs is home to restaurants, crafts shops, and inns that serve the needs of modern-day pilgrims.

DIRECTIONS TO THE START

From N.C. 16, go north on the Blue Ridge Parkway for 2.5 miles to the Northwest Trading Post, located at Milepost 258.6. You can leave your vehicle in the parking lot at the trading post. Glendale Springs is about 23 miles from Wilkesboro and 13 miles from West Jefferson.

DISTANCE

23.3 miles

CHALLENGE

⊛ ⊛ What's a pilgrimage without a little pain? This route has plenty of hilly terrain.

ROAD CONDITIONS AND CAUTIONS

The roads on this route are generally in good condition. The 0.3-mile stretch of dirt road near the end of the ride should be avoided during and after wet weather. U.S. 221 and N.C. 16 are busy roads; exercise caution as you make left turns on these highways.

CUES

0.0	Turn **right** out of the Northwest Trading Post's parking area onto the Blue Ridge Parkway and head south.
2.5	Turn **left** onto the ramp for N.C. 16 North.
2.6	Turn **right** at the stop sign onto N.C. 16 and head north toward West Jefferson.
3.0	Turn **left** onto N.C. 163.
8.5	Turn **left** onto Nettle Knob Road (S.R. 1147).
10.1	Turn **right** at the stop sign to continue on Nettle Knob Road.

13.1   Turn **right** at the stop sign onto U.S. 221 North.

13.5   Turn **left** at the traffic signal onto U.S. 221 Business/ N.C. 194.

13.6   Turn **left** at the traffic signal onto Beaver Creek School Road.

14.1   Turn **right** into the parking lot to visit St. Mary's Episcopal Church. Turn **left** out of the parking lot back onto Beaver Creek School Road.

14.6   Turn **right** at the traffic signal onto U.S. 221 Business/ N.C. 194.

14.7   Go **straight** at the traffic signal onto N.C. 163.

17.5   Turn **left** at North Beaver Baptist Church onto Boggs Road (S.R. 1159).

21.5   Turn **left** onto Glendale School Road (S.R. 1160).

23.0   Turn **right** at the stop sign onto S.R. 1161. Holy Trinity Episcopal Church is located at this intersection.

23.1   Turn **left** at the Glendale Springs Inn onto Trading Post Road (S.R. 1632), then go **straight** across N.C. 16 at the stop sign.

23.3   Turn **right** into the parking lot at the Northwest Trading Post to end the ride.

Highest Elevation

3,248 feet on the Blue Ridge Parkway near the Jumpinoff Rock Overlook, two miles into the ride

Lowest Elevation

2,715 feet at the low-water bridge over the New River, 21.1 miles into the ride

Food and Services

Restrooms are available at the Northwest Trading Post. Several country stores are located along the route. You'll find

Elevation Profile

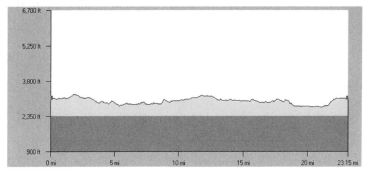

© 2002 DeLorme (www.delorme.com) *Topo USA* ® 4.0

a variety of fast-food options in West Jefferson near the intersection of U.S. 221 and N.C. 163. Glendale Springs has a sandwich shop, a bakery, and the elegant Glendale Springs Inn and Restaurant.

ROADSIDE ATTRACTIONS

St. Mary's Episcopal Church in West Jefferson is a simple mountain church that houses numerous pieces of religious art, including three frescoes by Ben Long. For more information, call 336-982-3076.

A large fresco of the Last Supper occupies the entire wall behind the altar at Holy Trinity Episcopal Church in Glendale Springs. Other religious art is in the church's basement. For more information, call 336-982-3076.

The Northwest Trading Post in Glendale Springs is a regional crafts outlet that offers handmade items, collectibles, antiques, and homemade goodies. For more information, call 336-982-2543.

OUTDOOR OPTIONS

Zaloo's Canoes near Glendale Springs offers canoeing and tubing on the New River. For more information, call 800-535-4027 or visit www.zaloos.com.

Big chainring, here I come! This photo shows the dramatic descent from the Lump on the Blue Ridge Parkway.

THE LUMP LOOP

SHORT TAKE

You can lump it *and* like it on this 25-mile loop past the Lump Overlook on the Blue Ridge Parkway. Amazing views, screaming descents, culture, and agriculture can all be found on this variety ride atop the Blue Ridge in Ashe and Wilkes Counties.

IN DEPTH

Would you rather pedal or piddle around? The Lump Loop can accommodate your wishes either way.

Hard-core road cyclists won't be disappointed. Two challenging uphills—a climb from Benge Gap to the Mount

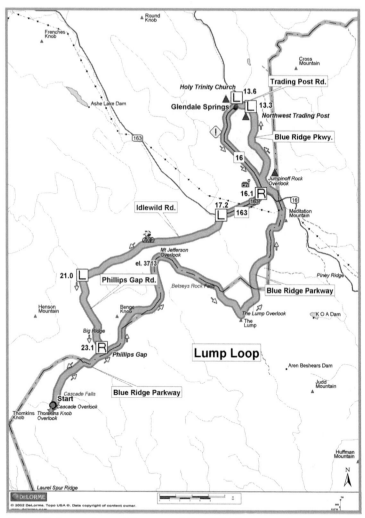

Round Knob

Frenches Knob

Cross Mountain

Ashe Lake Dam

163

Holy Trinity Church

Trading Post Rd.

L 13.6

L 13.3

Glendale Springs

Northwest Trading Post

Blue Ridge Pkwy.

16

Jumpinoff Rock Overlook

16.1 R

163

16

Idlewild Rd.

17.2 L

163

Meditation Mountain

Mt Jefferson Overlook

el. 3713

21.0 L

Phillips Gap Rd.

Betseys Rock Falls

Piney Ridge

Henson Mountain

Benge Knob

Blue Ridge Parkway

The Lump Overlook

K O A Dam

The Lump

Big Ridge

23.1 R

Phillips Gap

Lump Loop

Aren Beshears Dam

Judd Mountain

Cascade Falls

Start

Blue Ridge Parkway

Cascade Overlook

Thomkins Knob

Thomkins Knob Overlook

Huffman Mountain

N

Laurel Spur Ridge

DeLORME

© 2002 DeLorme. Topo USA ®. Data copyright of content owner.
www.delorme.com

© 2002 DeLorme (www.delorme.com) *Topo USA ® 4.0*

Jefferson Overlook and the ascent up Phillips Gap Road back to Cascades Park—bookend the ride. In between, type-A riders can hammer up a series of undulating hills on the ridge top and in the valley below.

Speedsters will appreciate the descents. North from the Lump Overlook, the Blue Ridge Parkway sheds almost 400 feet over about a mile in a smooth, swooping descent that offers commanding views of the foothills below. After a short uphill, the parkway does it all over again with a second cliff-side descent. Thanks to good road conditions and the artfully planned track of the roadway, these downhills don't demand excessive caution. Pedal hard, then tuck in and see how fast you can go as the foothills streak by below you.

The route even serves up a short stretch of relatively flat terrain along Idlewild Road that's perfect for a paceline.

So much for the pedalers. What's in it for the piddlers?

The Lump Loop offers easy hiking, crafts shopping, renowned religious art, and plenty of places to eat.

Short, leg-stretching trails are available at several spots along the route, including Cascades Park, Jumpinoff Rock, and the Lump. The Lump is a prominent lumplike hill along the crest of the Blue Ridge. It's a short walk from the Lump pull-off to the top of a large, open pasture. This is a great place to fly a kite, hang out with the cattle, and enjoy a broad view of the Yadkin River Valley and the Brushy Mountains. Just past N.C. 16, it's a mile round-trip walk amidst the oaks and galax to Jumpinoff Rock, a precipice on a knife's edge of the Blue Ridge. A quick hike at the end of the ride leads to the Cascades, a small waterfall where Falls Creek plunges down the side of the mountain, headed for the foothills far below. It seems

The Blue Ridge Parkway near Glendale Springs

like hiking might be the last thing a person would want to do during or after a strenuous bike ride, but I've found that light hiking uses the legs in a different fashion from biking and actually provides a nice stretch.

The small mountain community of Glendale Springs offers plenty of places to piddle around, too. The Northwest Trading Post is a regional crafts outlet featuring homemade products from 11 counties in the High Country. Who needs energy gel when you can get carbohydrate-rich fudge here? The Greenhouse Crafts Store, just off the route near the Glendale Springs Inn, has a variety of gift items. Glendale Springs is also home to Ben Long's famed fresco of the Last Supper, housed in historic Holy Trinity Episcopal Church; see "The Tour de Frescoes" for details. Since many of the thousands of pilgrims who come to view the fresco are hungry, Glendale Springs has a variety of places to eat. Mountain Music Jamboree, located near Glendale Springs on N.C. 16, has mountain music and dancing on weekends.

Considering all that Glendale Springs has to offer, it may make sense to begin and end the ride there. To do so, follow the alternative road directions to the Northwest Trading Post and pick up the "Cues" from mile 13.3 at Trading Post Road.

DIRECTIONS TO THE START

From Boone, head south on U.S. 421 to the Deep Gap entrance to the Blue Ridge Parkway. Follow the parkway north for 4.1 miles to the Cascades Picnic Area at E. B. Jeffress Park.

From Wilkesboro and the Piedmont, go north on U.S. 421 to the first Blue Ridge Parkway entrance, located at Deep Gap. Take the parkway north for 4.1 miles to the Cascades Picnic Area.

To start the ride in Glendale Springs, take the Blue Ridge Parkway north from N.C. 16 for 2.5 miles to the Northwest Trading Post, located at Milepost 258.6.

You can leave your vehicle in the parking lot at E. B. Jeffress Park, located at Milepost 271.9 on the parkway. If you'll be starting the ride in Glendale Springs, you can leave your vehicle in the parking lot at the Northwest Trading Post.

Note that daytime parking is permitted at parkway overlooks and shoulders, but don't block gates or leave your vehicle overnight.

DISTANCE

25.2 miles

CHALLENGE

✪✪ You'll take your lumps on this hilly ride, but there's nothing outrageously steep.

ROAD CONDITIONS AND CAUTIONS

The roads on this route are smooth surfaced and in good repair. N.C. 16 from N.C. 163 to Glendale Springs is busy, but a widening project has made it safer for cyclists. Parkway regulations require cyclists to ride single file.

CUES

0.0	Turn **right** out of the parking lot at E. B. Jeffress Park onto the Blue Ridge Parkway and head north.
13.3	Turn **left** at the Northwest Trading Post (Milepost 258.6) onto Trading Post Road (S.R. 1632).
13.6	Turn **left** at the stop sign onto N.C. 16 South.
16.1	Turn **right** onto N.C. 163.
17.2	Turn **left** onto Idlewild Road (S.R. 1003).
21.0	Turn **left** onto Phillips Gap Road (S.R. 1168).
23.1	Turn **right** at the stop sign onto the Blue Ridge Parkway and head south.

25.2   Turn **left** into the Cascades parking lot.

Highest Elevation

3,713 feet near the Mount Jefferson Overlook, 4.8 miles into the ride

Lowest Elevation

2,843 feet on N.C. 16 south of Glendale Springs, 14.4 miles into the ride

Food and Services

Water and restrooms are available seasonally at E. B. Jeffress Park and at the Northwest Trading Post. Restaurants are located at Benge Gap (four miles from the Cascades Picnic Area), in Glendale Springs, and near the junction of N.C. 16 and N.C. 163.

Elevation Profile

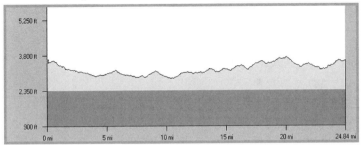

© 2002 DeLorme (www.delorme.com) *Topo USA* ® 4.0

ROADSIDE ATTRACTIONS

E. B. Jeffress Park encompasses 600 acres of mountain fields and forests. A pioneer log cabin and an old-time church are located on the grounds not far from the Cascades parking lot.

The Northwest Trading Post, located in Glendale Springs at Milepost 258.6 on the Blue Ridge Parkway, is a regional crafts outlet that offers handmade items, collectibles, antiques, and homemade goodies. For more information, call 336-982-2543.

Holy Trinity Episcopal Church in Glendale Springs is a historic mountain church that houses numerous pieces of religious art, including a large fresco of the Last Supper by Ben Long. The church is always open. For more information, call 336-982-3076.

Mountain Music Jamboree is located on N.C. 16 in Glendale Springs. It is said that "you can sit and grin or jump right in" at this family-oriented mountain-music and dance hall. For more information, call 336-384-4079 or visit www.mountainmusicjamboree.com.

OUTDOOR OPTIONS

Short hiking trails are located on the Blue Ridge Parkway at the Cascades, the Lump, and Jumpinoff Rock. Bicycles are not allowed on parkway trails.

THE DAMASCUS, VIRGINIA, AREA

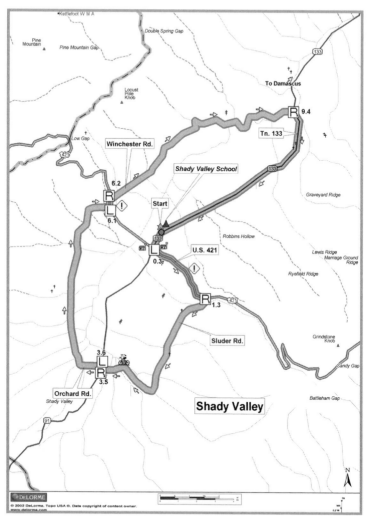

Kettlefoot W M A

Pine Mountain

Pine Mountain Gap

Double Spring Gap

To Damascus

133

Locust
Pole
Knob

Low Gap

R 9.4

421

Winchester Rd.

Tn. 133

133

6.2

Shady Valley School

Graveyard Ridge

R
L !

6.1

Start

Robbins Hollow

Lewis Ridge

Marriage Ground
Ridge

L

U.S. 421

Ryefield Ridge

0.3

!

R 1.3

421

Sluder Rd.

Grindstone
Knob

Sandy Gap

3.6

L

R

3.5

Orchard Rd.

Shady Valley

Shady Valley

Battleham Gap

91

N

DeLORME

© 2002 DeLorme, Topo USA ®. Data copyright of content owner.
www.delorme.com

© 2002 DeLorme (www.delorme.com) *Topo USA* ® 4.0

Cruising down a quiet country lane

THE SHADY VALLEY SOJOURN

Short Take

You'll tour a unique part of the High Country on this jaunt through the highest cove valley in Tennessee. The Shady Valley loop offers miles of level riding down quiet country lanes past farms, forests, and rare upland bogs. Wildlife abounds in this broad, bowl-like valley. If the 12-mile ride around the perimeter of Shady Valley isn't enough, the loop may easily be extended to form a scenic 33-mile route.

In Depth

Rimmed on three sides by high mountains, Shady Valley is

one of the most picturesque and peaceful spots in the Southern highlands. The valley is walled by two parallel mountain ranges—the Iron Mountains to the southeast and Holston Mountain to the northwest. Cross Mountain, located to the southwest, joins the two ridge lines to hem in the wide, four-mile-by-10-mile valley. High hills are almost always on the horizon on this ride.

Shady Valley's name is somewhat misleading. The valley is broad and open today, a mix of pastures, tobacco plots, hayfields, and horse farms. It was shady long ago, when it was covered by a dense forest in the days before white settlement began. Native American relics have been found along Beaverdam Creek, the stream that splits the big valley down the middle.

This isn't your typical mountain valley. It's home to several small bogs, a type of wetland quite rare in the highland South. Bogs are characterized by acidic waters, spongy peat deposits, and floors covered with thick carpets of sphagnum moss. They're most commonly found in formerly glaciated areas of New England and Canada. The Shady Valley bogs, once extensive, were largely drained by a federal soil-conservation project in the 1960s. Livestock now grazes on land where cranberries once grew. The Nature Conservancy is working with private landowners in the valley to restore the bogs by closing artificial drainage systems.

Fortunately, there's little to bog down cyclists riding through this serene valley. Only two hills of any size intrude on the level cruising here. The ride's biggest climb comes at the start. It's a gradual one-mile ascent on U.S. 421 South to the high point of the ride at the intersection with Sluder Road, elevation 3,038 feet. Once on Sluder Road, it's an easy downhill glide for

Riding on the "edge"— Wildlife abounds in the valley where field and forest meet.

several miles past pastures, orchards, and views of the mountains beyond.

Across Tenn. 91, the route skirts the edge of the valley on Orchard Road, a level country lane. About a mile up the road, you'll pass the Jesse Jenkins Cranberry Bog, a small tract managed by the Nature Conservancy. Look for deer and wild turkeys in the fields adjoining the hillside forests. Waterfowl frequent the wetlands below.

After a quick jog on U.S. 421 North, it's on to Winchester Road and a spin along the western fringe of the valley. Big fields of burley tobacco flank the road. The crop is air-dried in barns in the fall. One of the old barns is so close to the road that it looks like a drive-thru smoke shop.

Winchester Road feeds into Gorman Gentry Road, the start of a mile-long downhill thrill ride along cascading Beaverdam Creek. Tall pines make this one of the shadiest places in Shady Valley.

The stop sign at Tenn. 133 marks the low point of the loop. As the creek rolls north, the route turns south for the last hill of the ride. It's less than a mile from the cool creek bottom back up to the open valley.

The ride begins and ends at a picnic area built by the local Ruritan Club. It's near Shady Valley School, a stately rock structure built during the Great Depression. The school, which once served more than 250 students, is down to 60 elementary-school children today, a testament to the High Country's dwindling ranks of farm families. The handsome school building is a point of local pride and the site of the annual Cranberry Festival. Cranberries aren't grown commercially here, but the community stages the festival the second full weekend in October to keep the memory of the bogs alive.

With just two real hills, some quiet country lanes, and loads of level land, this loop is a great route for casual riders. More serious cyclists can extend the ride by adding the stretch of Tenn. 133 from Gorman Gentry Road to Damascus, Virginia. This road hugs the banks of Beaverdam Creek through Cherokee National Forest, tracing the tracks of a century-old railroad line. Tenn. 133 boasts what may be the world's shortest tunnel, a passage through jagged Backbone Rock that's just 14 feet long! Shady Valley is about 700 feet higher than Damascus, so if you prefer to delay your gratification, you can begin the ride in Damascus, ride upstream to Shady Valley, do the loop, and then enjoy an easy spin back downstream. This lasso-shaped extended route offers 33 miles of scenic splendor.

DIRECTIONS TO THE START

From Boone, North Carolina, go north on U.S. 421 approximately 35 miles; you'll cross the Tennessee line en route to Shady

Valley. Turn right at the flashing light onto Tenn. 133 North. Drive 0.3 mile and turn left into the Ruritan Picnic Area, located near Shady Valley School. The ride begins here.

DISTANCE

11.9 miles

CHALLENGE

✪ This short ride has loads of level riding and only two hills of any length.

ROAD CONDITIONS AND CAUTIONS

All the roads on this route are smoothly surfaced and in good condition. Watch for traffic on U.S. 421 and Tenn. 133.

Shady Valley is rimmed on three sides by high mountain ridges.

Cues

0.0   Turn **right** out of the Ruritan Picnic Area onto Tenn. 133 South.

0.3   Turn **left** at the flashing light onto U.S. 421 and head south toward Mountain City.

1.3   Turn **right** onto Sluder Road.

3.5   Turn **right** at the stop sign onto Tenn. 91 North.

3.6   Make a **quick left** onto Orchard Road.

4.1   Go **straight**. Do not turn left on Orchard Road.

6.1   Turn **left** at the stop sign onto U.S. 421 North.

6.2   Make a **quick right** onto Winchester Road at the Presbyterian church.

9.4   Turn **right** at the stop sign onto Tenn. 133 South.

11.9   You will return to the Ruritan Picnic Area.

Highest Elevation

3,038 feet near the intersection of U.S. 421 and Sluder Road, 1.3 miles into the ride

Elevation Profile

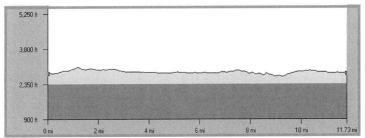

© 2002 DeLorme (www.delorme.com) *Topo USA ® 4.0*

LOWEST ELEVATION

2,661 feet near the intersection of Gorman Gentry Road and Tenn.133, some 9.4 miles into the ride

FOOD AND SERVICES

Several country stores and a café are located at the intersection of U.S. 421 and Tenn. 133/Tenn. 91.

OUTDOOR OPTIONS

Beaverdam Creek offers great fly-fishing.

The Appalachian Trail crosses Holston Mountain west of the valley.

Backbone Rock Recreation Area, eight miles north of Shady Valley on Tenn. 133, offers a picnic area, hiking trails, a waterfall, and cascading Beaverdam Creek.

Big view near Skull's Gap

THE ROAD TO DAMASCUS

Short Take

So you think Damascus, Virginia, is just for mountain bikes? You'll see the light on this challenging 38-mile road ride through the peaceful valleys and high mountains east of town. This route is a combo plate of High Country road cycling. It includes hearty helpings of flat valley cruising and arduous climbing, served up with a wild white-knuckle descent and a curvy creek-side spin through scenic Jefferson National Forest.

In Depth

Damascus is a tiny town big on the outdoors.

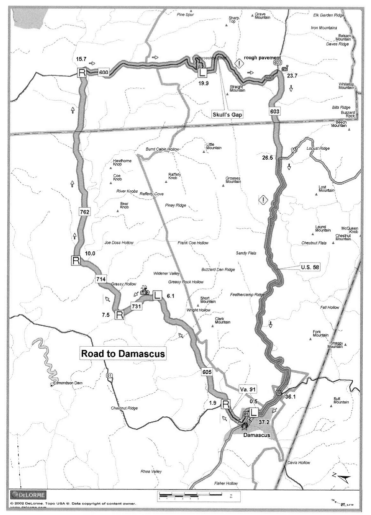

Road to Damascus

Skull's Gap

Damascus

© 2002 DeLorme (www.delorme.com) *Topo USA* ® 4.0

The Appalachian Trail, the Virginia Creeper rail-trail, a couple of tumbling trout streams, and two national forests all converge at Damascus, the self-proclaimed "friendliest town on the Appalachian Trail."

The AT runs right through the middle of downtown Damascus. White blazes on utility poles and the sidewalk mark the route. Each year, this town of 1,000 hosts hordes of hikers, especially during the annual Trail Days celebration in mid-May. That's when backpackers attempting the entire 2,150-mile Georgia-to-Maine trail come to town for a raucous outdoor gathering.

Most days, though, hikers are outnumbered by bikers, thanks to the Virginia Creeper Trail. Damascus is the midway point of the 34-mile unpaved rail-trail, which follows the route of the once-grand, now-defunct Virginia-Carolina Railroad. Several outfitters shuttle cyclists to the trail's high point at Whitetop Station, sending them off on a 17-mile downhill jaunt to Damascus.

Large tracts of national forest abut Damascus, which lies at the foot of Virginia's highest mountains. The clear, rushing streams flowing from those peaks lure anglers. The network of trails and forest roads through the high mountains east of town draws hard-core mountain bikers and the horsey set.

All this outdoor activity has changed the face of once-sleepy Damascus. The town too small for a Wal-Mart has a bike shop and an outfitter that put larger towns to shame. On pretty days, two-wheel vehicles seem to outnumber four-wheel ones, as bushed bikers spill off the Virginia Creeper Trail into town in search of refreshments.

Road cyclists are a rare breed here, easily outnumbered by the masses of off-road bikers tooling down the famous trail. But here's a secret: Damascus has some great road biking. The town is the hub of a network of scenic, lightly traveled secondary roads ideal for cycling. It's even traversed by Bike Route 76, the original coast-to-coast Bikecentennial route.

This loop is a sampler of some of the best road riding the area has to offer.

After a spin through downtown Damascus, the route escapes to the open hill-and-dale country north of town. Widener Valley Road rolls through a series of undulating hills, climbing and falling without gaining much elevation. The hayfields are bordered by tall, wooded knobs. Once-proud farmhouses lie abandoned, giving the area a melancholy feel.

A quick downhill scoot along Bucks Branch leads to the South Fork of the Holston River and some easy pedaling down a flat, quiet country lane. South Fork River Road follows the stream for several miles as it winds among steep, forested hills and broad pastures.

Love's Mill Road rolls along a ridge above the river, offering views of the valley and "the Knobs," a series of lumpy hills flanking the river. Beyond the Knobs is a long, straight mountain range. Take a good look at that far-off mountain wall; you've got to go up and over it to complete the loop.

At an elevation of 2,086 feet, the route departs the broad river valley to climb alongside St. Clair Creek. The bold creek dwindles over the five miles from the South Fork of the Holston to the top of the ridge at Skulls Gap. This ominously named gap offers a killer climb. Most of the steep stuff is stacked in the last two miles of the 1,600-foot ascent. Unmarked Skulls Gap isn't much to see, but an overlook just shy of the top offers a sweeping view of the broad valley below. The view, like the grind up the mountain, is breathtaking.

It's a Dr. Jekyll and Mr. Hyde descent from Skulls Gap. The modern highway near the top of the mountain plunges in a straight, smooth path that just begs to be ridden fast. Speeds of 45 miles per hour or more are easily attainable here. Then, suddenly, the smooth pavement gives way to ruts and bumps as the straight road morphs into a slithering slalom along the shady banks of Little Laurel Creek.

Once off the mountain, the loop joins the TransAmerica bike route, following the path of Big Laurel Creek through a high mountain valley. (If Skulls Gap wasn't enough climbing for you, take a left on Va. 600, tack on the 5.4-mile climb to Elk Garden, and return to the valley.) The pedaling is easy along this straight stretch near Konnarock, a once-bustling logging town that's shrunk to a mere village today. Lofty Whitetop Mountain looms to the left over the valley.

The ride's home stretch follows U.S. 58. This road may be part of the federal system, but it's hardly a highway. U.S. 58 is narrow and winding. It snakes along the side of Straight Mountain, tracing the twisting paths of two creeks as they tumble downhill toward town.

A lack of shoulders, limited sight distance, and precious few places to pull off make U.S. 58 sound like a cyclist's nightmare. Despite all that, it is actually a road biker's dream. The short rise out of Konnarock along the southwest edge of Straight Mountain is gradual and snaky; fit riders can carve the curves almost as fast as the cars do. Bear Tree Gap marks the beginning of a seven-mile descent back to Damascus. You'll zip through turn after turn as the road rushes along Straight Branch and Whitetop Laurel Creek, shedding 1,000 feet in elevation; vehicle traffic can't get through the turns much faster than you can. A road rider here is one with the water, rushing rapidly down the road in time with the surging stream, then cruising a bit more slowly as the creek widens in the valley near town. This stretch through Jefferson National Forest is an outdoor paradise. You'll zoom by anglers teasing trout in Whitetop Laurel Creek and families pedaling along the Virginia Creeper Trail.

The route ends with a quick victory lap down Laurel Avenue in Damascus, the main drag that's part federal highway and part Appalachian Trail.

DIRECTIONS TO THE START

From Boone, North Carolina, take U.S. 421 North to Mountain City, Tennessee. At Mountain City, turn right on Tenn. 91, which intersects U.S. 58 just across the Virginia border. Turn left on U.S. 58 and follow it down Laurel Avenue in Damascus. Turn left just past the bridge over Beaverdam Creek onto South Beaverdam Avenue. You can leave your vehicle at the town park at the corner of South Beaverdam Avenue and West Laurel Avenue; look for the red caboose.

DISTANCE

37.7 miles

CHALLENGE

⊗ ⊗ ∅ The steep climb to Skulls Gap is the ride's only major ascent.

ROAD CONDITIONS AND CAUTIONS

The pavement quality varies widely on this route. Be especially careful for the abrupt transition to rough pavement on the descent from Skulls Gap. U.S. 58 can be busy; since it offers few good spots for vehicles to pass, ride fast and be prepared to pull over to let traffic by.

CUES

0.0   Turn **right** from the park onto U.S. 58 East (West Laurel Avenue).

0.5   Turn **left** onto Va. 91 North.

1.9   Turn **right** onto Va. 605 (Widener Valley Road).

6.1   Turn **left** at the bottom of the hill onto Va. 731 (Bucks Branch Road).

7.5   Turn **right** just past the small bridge onto Va. 714 (South Fork River Road).

10.0   Turn **right** at the stop sign onto Va. 762 (Love's Mill Road).

15.7   Turn **right** at the stop sign onto Va. 600 (St. Clair Creek Road).

18.4   Go **straight** at Ramblewood Lane onto Old Va. 600.

19.9   Turn **left** at the stop sign onto Whitetop Road.

21.5   You'll reach Skulls Gap, elevation 3,689 feet. Caution:
        Road conditions deteriorate on the descent.

23.7   Go **straight** at the junction with Va. 603. The elevation
        here is 3,071 feet.

23.8   Go **straight** onto Va. 603 and head west toward
        Konnarock.

26.5   Go **straight** onto U.S. 58 West.

36.1   You'll reach a junction with Va. 91. Go **straight** at the
        stop sign on U.S. 58 West.

37.2   Turn **left** onto Laurel Avenue to follow U.S. 58 West.

37.7   Turn **left** onto South Beaverdam Avenue to return to
        the park.

*A curvy creekside
cruise on U.S. 58*

Elevation Profile

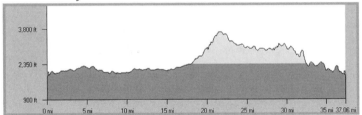

© 2002 DeLorme (www.delorme.com) *Topo USA* ® *4.0*

HIGHEST ELEVATION

3,694 feet at Skulls Gap, 21.5 miles into the ride

LOWEST ELEVATION

1,905 feet at the start and finish in Damascus

FOOD AND SERVICES

Damascus has stores, bike shops, and restaurants. Two country stores are located near the intersection of Va. 600 and Va. 603 at the bottom of the descent from Skulls Gap, about 24 miles into the ride.

OUTDOOR OPTIONS

The area offers great mountain biking, hiking, and fly-fishing. The Virginia Creeper Trail is an excellent off-road cycling experience for groups and families. Tom Horsch at Adventure Damascus on Laurel Avenue is well acquainted with the area's many outdoor options.

NORTHEAST OF BOONE

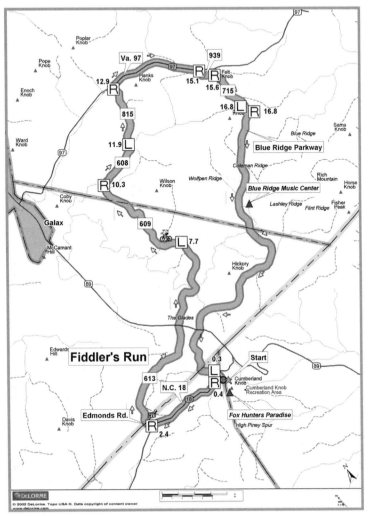

Va. 97

939

12.9 **R**

Hanks Knob

15.1 **R** 15.6 **R** Felt Knob

815

11.9 **L**

608

10.3 **R**

715

16.8 **L** **R** 16.8 Knob

Blue Ridge Parkway

Coleman Ridge

Blue Ridge Music Center

609

7.7 **L**

Wolfpen Ridge

Wilson Knob

The Glades

Fiddler's Run

0.3

Start

613

L **R**

Cumberland Knob

N.C. 18

0.4

Cumberland Knob Recreation Area

Fox Hunters Paradise

Edmonds Rd.

High Piney Spur

2.4 **R**

Galax

Poplar Knob

Pope Knob

Enoch Knob

Ward Knob

Coby Knob

McCamant Hill

Edwards Hill

Davis Knob

Blue Ridge

Sams Knob

Rich Mountain

Horse Knob

Lashley Ridge Flint Ridge Fisher Peak

Hickory Knob

97

© 2002 DeLorme. Topo USA ®. Data copyright of content owner.
www.delorme.com

© 2002 DeLorme (www.delorme.com) *Topo USA* ® 4.0

Pasture and pines on the Parkway

FIDDLER'S RUN

SHORT TAKE

You'll fiddle around on the back roads of the Blue Ridge on this 25-mile loop. The "Fiddler's Run" route links Cumberland Knob Recreation Area, the oldest facility on the Blue Ridge Parkway, with the Blue Ridge Music Center, the parkway's newest attraction. It starts just across the state line in North Carolina and meanders along country lanes south of Galax, Virginia, a town famous for mountain music.

IN DEPTH

The hills near Galax are alive with the sound of music. Not just any music, mind you, but mountain music. Acoustic music played hard and fast on the fiddle, banjo, guitar, and stand-up bass. The high, lonesome sound of ancient ballads sung un-accompanied. Gospel music performed in tight four-part harmony. If it's real mountain music you crave, there's no better place to hear it than Galax.

Thousands flock to town in August for the annual Old Time Fiddlers Convention. Radio station WBRF offers free mountain-music concerts Friday nights in the historic Rex Theatre. The Ruritan Club in tiny Fairview south of Galax stages an ambitious series of concerts featuring local bands and mountain-music legends like Ralph Stanley.

The Blue Ridge Parkway's latest attraction, the Blue Ridge Music Center, will certainly cement the area's reputation as a hotbed of mountain music. The center, situated on a knoll above Chestnut Creek at Milepost 213, is being built in several phases. An amphitheater and an instrument builder's shop are already open. A museum on the same site will preserve the rich history of mountain music with films, exhibits, and a listening library.

The rhythms of this acoustic art form are perfect for cycling. Pick any up-tempo tune, get it stuck in your head, and hit the road. If you pedal in time to the music in your mind, you'll be spinning like Lance in no time.

The route begins near the North Carolina-Virginia line and winds through the hills of Grayson and Carroll Counties in Virginia. This area atop the Blue Ridge is open and rolling, creased by a series of creeks flowing toward the New River. Except for the elevation, the riding here is much like in the rural foothills several thousand feet below. It's uphill and downhill, again and again, over a series of open knolls.

Pastures and pines are the dominant features of the landscape. Cattle, horses, and sheep graze in broad, green fields. Tall Virginia pines tower over the roadside. This distinctive tree is portrayed on the official symbol of the Blue Ridge Parkway.

Large dogs are another feature of the route. Big, shaggy mutts snooze in front of nearly every farmhouse along Coal Creek Road and Shepherd Place. Be vigilant and pedal quietly. Heaven help you if you wake them up!

The stretch of the route on the Blue Ridge Parkway is a quiet spin through the back country of the Virginia highlands. This portion of the parkway is several miles north of the knife's edge of the ridge, so there are no big views into the Piedmont below. Instead, the parkway runs through fields bordered with split-rail fences. Fisher's Peak towers over tracts of mixed forest.

For a big view, pedal back into North Carolina. Less than a mile past Cumberland Knob Recreation Area, you'll reach the Fox Hunter's Paradise Overlook, located at Milepost 218.6. From this 2,800-foot perch, it's easy to spot bumpy Pilot Mountain and the Sauratown range protruding from the expansive Piedmont below.

DIRECTIONS TO THE START

From Interstate 77, take Exit 100 and drive north on N.C. 89 for 12 miles to N.C. 18. Turn left onto N.C. 18 and go a half-mile to the Blue Ridge Parkway. Head south on the parkway. The parking lot at Cumberland Knob Recreation Area (Milepost 217.5) is on the left after 0.3 mile. The recreation area is about 17 miles east of Sparta, North Carolina; 21 miles west of Mount Airy, North Carolina; and nine miles south of Galax, Virginia. Daytime parking is permitted at parkway overlooks and shoulders, but don't block gates or leave your vehicle overnight.

DISTANCE

25 miles

CHALLENGE

✖ ☭ The hills on this route are generally short and not too steep.

ROAD CONDITIONS AND CAUTIONS

Road conditions vary from the smooth asphalt of Va. 97 and the Blue Ridge Parkway to patchy pavement on some of the country lanes. Canines, not cars, are the biggest safety concern on the lightly traveled secondary roads. Parkway regulations require cyclists to ride single file.

CUES

0.0   Turn **right** out of the Cumberland Knob Recreation Area parking lot onto the Blue Ridge Parkway and head north.

0.3   Turn **left** onto the N.C. 18 ramp.

0.4   Turn **right** at the stop sign onto N.C. 18 and head west toward Sparta.

Back roads pass through quiet farm country.

2.4   Turn **right** onto Edmonds Road (S.R. 1142).

2.6   You'll reach the Virginia state line and begin Va. 613 (Edmonds Road).

5.3   Go **straight** at the stop sign at Va. 89. Continue on Va. 613 (Snow Hill Road).

7.7   Turn **left** at the stop sign onto Va. 609 (Peaks Mountain Road).

10.3   Turn **right** at the stop sign onto Va. 608 (Coal Creek Road).

11.3   Bear **left** at the fork onto Va. 815 (Shepherd Place).

12.9   Turn **right** at the stop sign onto Va. 97 (Pipers Gap Road).

15.1   Turn **right** onto Va. 939 (Cockerham Loop).

15.6   Turn **right** onto Va. 715 (Coleman Lane).

16.8   Turn **left** at the bottom of the hill to continue on Va. 715, then make a **quick right** at the stop sign onto the Blue Ridge Parkway and head south.

20.3   You'll reach the entrance to the Blue Ridge Music Center.

25.0   Turn **left** into the parking lot at Cumberland Knob Recreation Area.

HIGHEST ELEVATION

3,027 feet at Felts Knob on Va. 715 (Coleman Lane), 15.9 miles into the ride

LOWEST ELEVATION

2,465 feet crossing a branch of Chestnut Creek on Va. 609 (Peaks Mountain Road), 8.1 miles into the ride

Elevation Profile

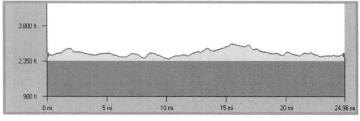

© 2002 DeLorme (www.delorme.com) *Topo USA* ® *4.0*

Food and Services

Restrooms are available at Cumberland Knob Recreation Area and the Blue Ridge Music Center. Both parkway attractions are open May through October. A country store and a restaurant are located at the intersection of N.C. 18 and Edmonds Road, 2.4 miles into the ride.

Roadside Attractions

The Blue Ridge Music Center (Milepost 213) is open seasonally. Its outdoor amphitheater and its instrument builder's shop are already in operation. A museum and a trail system are planned. Outdoor concerts coordinated by the National Council for the Traditional Arts are offered during warm weather. For more information, visit www.ncta.net/blueridge.html.

Outdoor Options

The 800-acre Cumberland Knob Recreation Area (Milepost 217.5) offers hiking and picnicking. A 15-minute loop trail leads to Cumberland Knob. The more challenging Gully Creek Trail is a two-hour loop that descends from the ridge into the Gully Creek Gorge. Bicycles are not allowed on any parkway trails.

An old farm on Glade Valley Road

GLADE VALLEY:
THE "LOST PROVINCE" LOOP

SHORT TAKE

This 33-mile loop combines the oldest stretch of the Blue Ridge Parkway with a scenic spin down some lightly traveled country roads in Alleghany County, North Carolina, an area so isolated that it was known for years as the "Lost Province." The ride begins and ends at the birthplace of the parkway, Cumberland Knob Recreation Area, just 13 miles from Interstate 77. It passes farms, forests, and two peaceful ponds.

IN DEPTH

This ride begins at Cumberland Knob, the place where, on September 11, 1935, ground was first broken for the Blue Ridge

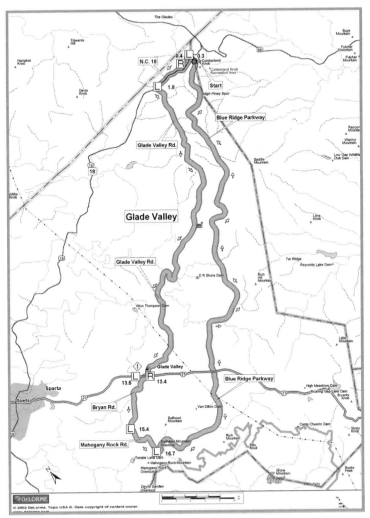

© 2002 DeLorme (www.delorme.com) *Topo USA* ® 4.0

Parkway. Construction commenced not far from the home of Robert "Muley Bob" Doughton, who just happened to be chairman of the House Ways and Means Committee at the time. Doughton's influence helped steer the parkway's route toward North Carolina; Tennessee politicians lobbied for a more westerly route that would have taken the federal project through the mountains of their state.

The locals were puzzled when the first bulldozers pushed dirt here. The mountain roads were so poor and travel so arduous that a "pleasure road" seemed mighty far-fetched. They soon warmed to the concept, though, thanks in part to the princely 30-cents-per-hour wage paid to parkway workers.

The Blue Ridge Parkway was the nation's first rural parkway and is still its longest. The 470-mile ridge-top road linking Shenandoah and Great Smoky Mountains National Parks was conceived primarily as a way to put men back to work during the Great Depression. It surely didn't occur to Senator Harry F. Byrd, who proposed the idea, or to President Franklin D. Roosevelt, who enthusiastically took it up, what a nirvana their parkway would be for cyclists.

Imagine a nice rural road for riding. Now, eliminate the big rigs and slow the traffic down. Take out the flashing signs, convenience stores, and utility lines that equate with "civilization." Add breathtaking views from the roadway, from strategically located pullouts, and from parks up to 6,000 acres in size. Throw in challenging climbs and dramatic descents, and you've got the Blue Ridge Parkway, the most beautiful highway in America.

This ride forms a large loop through the farm country of Alleghany County, an area that's always been off the beaten path. Alleghany, the county with the lowest population density

A peaceful pond on the Parkway

in northwestern North Carolina, has plenty of rural country-side for cyclists to explore. As you pass through its dairy country on this ride, it might seem that cows outnumber people here. The large, open pastures on the wide plateau north of the Blue Ridge allow expansive views of the surrounding mountains.

The loop returns to the Blue Ridge Parkway after a short, steep climb. The Mahogany Rock Overlook, just up the road to the right from where you reenter the parkway, is a prime spot from which to watch the annual migration of broad-winged hawks in late August and early September. Unlike other hawks, broad wings migrate en masse. The high-flying hawks appear in the distance 100 or more strong in soaring groups called kettles. The kettles catch the updraft over the Blue Ridge during the annual migration, much to the delight of birders, who station themselves at overlooks along this stretch of the parkway to see the spectacle.

The ride hits its high point after a mile or so on the parkway. Then it's a nice downhill and a relatively easy cruise back to Cumberland Knob Recreation Area. The big views of the first several miles of the parkway recede as the road steers away from the ridge. Two old millponds (near Mileposts 230 and 225) are scenic spots to take a rest, but given the fairly level terrain in this stretch, you may feel too good to stop.

DIRECTIONS TO THE START

From Interstate 77, take Exit 100 and drive north on N.C. 89 for 12 miles to N.C. 18. Turn left onto N.C. 18 and go a half-mile to the Blue Ridge Parkway. Head south on the parkway. The parking lot for Cumberland Knob Recreation Area (Milepost 217.5) is on the left after 0.3 mile. The recreation area is about 17 miles east of Sparta, North Carolina; 21 miles west of Mount Airy, North Carolina; and nine miles south of Galax, Virginia. Daytime parking is permitted at parkway overlooks and shoulders, but don't block gates or leave your vehicle overnight.

DISTANCE

33.2 miles

CHALLENGE

⊗⊗ The short, steep ascent to the parkway on Mahogany Rock Road is the ride's toughest climb. The stretch of the parkway past U.S. 21 is one of the scenic road's gentlest sections.

ROAD CONDITIONS AND CAUTIONS

The section of the Blue Ridge Parkway and the secondary roads on this route are in good condition. Use caution as you ride the short distance on the heavily traveled U.S. 21. Parkway regulations require cyclists to ride single file.

CUES

0.0   Turn **right** out of the parking lot at Cumberland Knob Recreation Area onto the Blue Ridge Parkway and head north.

0.3   Turn **left** onto the N.C. 18 ramp.

0.4   Turn **right** at the stop sign onto N.C. 18 and head west toward Sparta.

1.8   Turn **left** at the Eastern Continental Divide sign onto Glade Valley Road (S.R. 1444).

13.0   Bear **left** entering the village of Glade Valley; stay on S.R. 1444.

13.4   Turn **right** at the stop sign onto U.S. 21 and head north toward Sparta. Caution: U.S. 21 is busy.

13.5   Make a **quick left** onto Bryan Road (S.R. 1113).

15.4   Turn **left** at the stop sign onto Mahogany Rock Road
        (S.R. 1115).

16.7   Turn **left** at the stop sign at the top of the steep hill to
        head north on the Blue Ridge Parkway.

33.2   Turn **right** into the parking lot at Cumberland Knob
        Recreation Area.

HIGHEST ELEVATION

3,288 feet on the Blue Ridge Parkway, 18 miles into the
ride

LOWEST ELEVATION

2,530 feet at Brush Creek on Glade Valley Road, 9.4 miles
into the ride

Elevation Profile

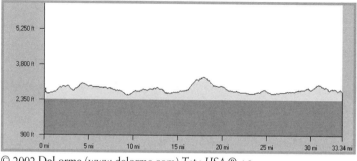

© 2002 DeLorme (www.delorme.com) *Topo USA* ® 4.0

FOOD AND SERVICES

Restrooms are available seasonally at Cumberland Knob Recreation Area. A country store is located on Glade Valley Road about eight miles into the ride. Buffalo Bob's carries drinks and snack items; the store is on the left at Milepost 232, about 19 miles into the ride.

OUTDOOR OPTIONS

The 800-acre Cumberland Knob Recreation Area (Milepost 217.5) offers hiking and picnicking. A 15-minute loop trail leads to Cumberland Knob. The more challenging Gully Creek Trail is a two-hour loop that descends from the ridge into the Gully Creek Gorge. Bicycles are not allowed on any parkway trails.

The Mahogany Rock Overlook, located on the right near Milepost 235, is a prime bird-watching site, especially during the fall hawk migration. To get to the overlook, turn right where the route intersects the parkway and ride one mile.

Bald is beautiful—open country abounds in Doughton Park.

A RIDE IN THE SKY: THE DOUGHTON PARK TOUR

SHORT TAKE

You'll experience one of the crown jewels of the Blue Ridge Parkway on this 36-mile out-and-back route. As the ride rolls along the high spine of Doughton Park, it offers sweeping views in all directions. Abundant wildlife, historic log cabins, a quiet millpond, broad, grassy balds, and rugged cliffs are all part of this road ride in the sky.

IN DEPTH

The Blue Ridge Parkway is one revolutionary road.

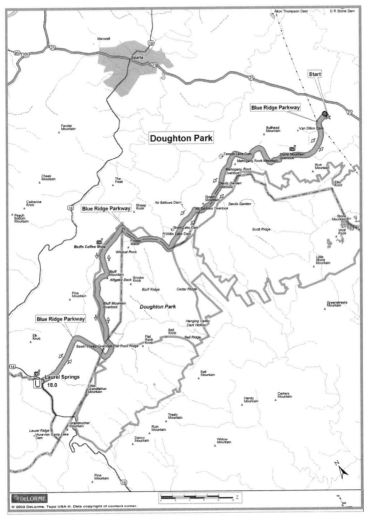

© 2002 DeLorme (www.delorme.com) *Topo USA* ® 4.0

It was built in an era when the average mountain road was a muddy, rutted path that forded streams, rather than crossing them on bridges. Then along came the parkway in the depths of the Great Depression, bringing a completely different concept of what a road could be. It wasn't just the smooth pavement and solid engineering. It was the whole concept that a road could exist for pleasure. The parkway was a road laid out not by buffalo or even pragmatic engineers, but by landscape architects, who turned the dull prose of point-A-to-point-B road making into poetry.

Stanley Abbott, the chief landscape architect involved in planning the parkway, visualized the great road as a movie. The Blue Ridge Parkway, in Abbott's conception, would be "the method by which the varied and countless scenes composing the Blue Ridge are unfolded, or as it were, projected to the visitor."

If the Doughton Park stretch of the parkway were a movie, which one would it be?

Top Gun

You won't reach supersonic speeds here, but hurtling downhill at 40 miles per hour atop two contact patches the size of postage stamps feels fast as a jet fighter. The sweeping views on this leg of the parkway make the ride seem like a low-altitude fly-by.

The Natural

The parkway runs along the rim of Doughton Park, a wedge-shaped, 6,000-acre tract of sweeping balds, rocky bluffs, hardwood forests, and deep bottom land. The park, the Blue Ridge

Miles of split-rail fences line the Parkway through Doughton Park.

Parkway's largest, is flanked by state game lands and Stone Mountain State Park. Unlike the section of the parkway between Boone and Blowing Rock, where homes keep sprouting like so many dandelions after a spring rain, this wild, unspoiled stretch of road is fairly free of human incursion. The road itself is so artfully laid out that it seems part of the landscape, not an intrusion upon it. Masses of migrating hawks swoop over the ridge each fall near the Mahogany Rock Overlook. Tadpoles turn into frogs each spring in the old millpond near U.S. 21. Deer gambol through the fields and forests, undeterred by the miles of split-rail fences lining the parkway. Even the stars shine brighter; dark-sky lovers gather here to watch meteor showers and other celestial events.

The Way We Were

The history of the area is portrayed at Brinegar Cabin, a living-history site with a pioneer garden and weaving demonstrations. The cabin, open seasonally, is just off the road at Milepost 238.5. Caudill Cabin, left behind by one of the hardy families who lived in the cove at the foot of the mountain, can be spied from a promontory near Bluffs Lodge.

The Agony and the Ecstasy

It's a climb to Doughton Park from either direction. From U.S. 21, three long ascents are broken by overlooks and short downhill respites. From the N.C. 18 side, it's a multimile slog from the valley at Laurel Springs to the first overlook at the western edge of the park. The views from the well-placed overlooks and the sheer exhilaration of the downhills make the pain of climbing well worth it. If you prefer more tangible rewards, stop at the coffee shop near Milepost 241 for some hot fruit cobbler.

A Walk to Remember

If you like to combine biking with hiking, this route's got you covered. Doughton Park is laced with 30 miles of trails along the ridge and into the deep cove below. Its broad balds are perfect for rambling without a trail. A spur road to the park's picnic area will take you to a large bald that offers commanding views of both sides of the Blue Ridge.

Ice Age

A large cliff along the roadway near the Alligator Back Overlook seeps water. During cold weather, this water freezes, forming huge icicles and ornate displays of ice.

The route described in the "Cues" is an out-and-back from U.S. 21 near Roaring Gap to N.C. 18 at Laurel Springs. It also can be started from the Laurel Springs end, which is closer to Boone and the heart of the High Country.

DIRECTIONS TO THE START

From Interstate 77, take Exit 83 and go north on U.S. 21 approximately 21 miles to the Blue Ridge Parkway. Drive south on the parkway for a half-mile to the Little Glade Pond Overlook, on the left. Daytime parking is permitted at parkway overlooks and shoulders, but don't block gates or leave your vehicle overnight.

DISTANCE

36 miles

CHALLENGE

⊗⊗You can expect plenty of climbing, but the grades aren't walk-your-bike steep.

ROAD CONDITIONS AND CAUTIONS

The Blue Ridge Parkway is well maintained, with only an occasional patch to mar the smooth surface. Traffic varies by season and time of day; weekends and the fall leaf season are the busiest times. Parkway regulations require cyclists to ride single file.

CUES

0.0   Turn **left** out of the Little Glade Pond Overlook onto the Blue Ridge Parkway and head south.

11.0   You'll reach the Bluffs Coffee Shop, elevation 3,720 feet. A spur road here leads to a view of Caudill Cabin and the large grassy area near the picnic grounds.

18.0   **Turn around** at the N.C. 18 overpass.

36.0   Turn **right** into the Little Glade Pond Overlook.

HIGHEST ELEVATION

3,744 feet near the Air Bellows Gap Overlook, seven miles and 29 miles into the ride

LOWEST ELEVATION

2,709 feet near Little Glade Creek at the start and finish

Elevation Profile

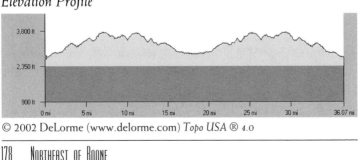

© 2002 DeLorme (www.delorme.com) *Topo USA* ® 4.0

View toward Sparta

FOOD AND SERVICES

Buffalo Bob's, just off the parkway at Milepost 232, has drinks and snack items. The Bluffs Coffee Shop and a small store, on the route at Milepost 241, are open seasonally. Bluffs Lodge, just off the parkway near Milepost 241, is also open seasonally. Several stores, a motel, and a restaurant are located just off the parkway on N.C. 18 North at Laurel Springs, 18 miles into the ride. Woody's Café and General Store in Laurel Springs is a curiosity shop well worth a short side trip; for information, call 336-359-2564.

ROADSIDE ATTRACTIONS

Brinegar Cabin is located at Milepost 238.5. Martin Brinegar built the cabin and outbuildings over a five-year period starting in 1885. Today, the cabin is the site of seasonal weaving and folklore demonstrations.

Caudill Cabin is located past Bluffs Lodge off the parkway

at Milepost 241. This cabin, tucked away at the foot of the Blue Ridge wall, was built by Martin Caudill in 1895. He and his large family lived for about 20 years in this small log structure situated 1,500 feet below the edge of Wildcat Rocks.

OUTDOOR OPTIONS

Doughton Park has more than 30 miles of hiking trails. Bicycles are not allowed on any parkway trails.

The Mahogany Rock Overlook, located at Milepost 235, is a prime bird-watching site, especially during the fall hawk migration.

The Foothills

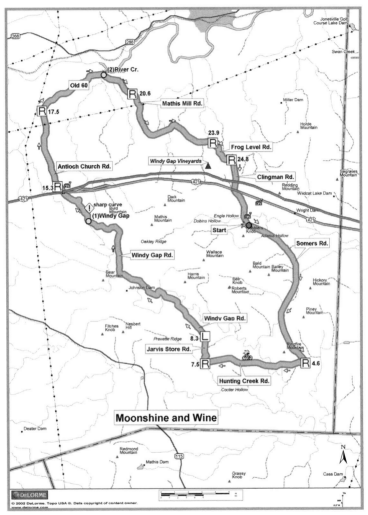

Moonshine and Wine

© 2002 DeLorme (www.delorme.com) *Topo USA* ® 4.0

Soaring down Somers Road

THE MOONSHINE AND WINE TOUR

SHORT TAKE

This 27-mile route loops through the old "Bootlegger Belt" of Wilkes County, North Carolina, where NASCAR legend Junior Johnson sharpened his driving skills running moonshine from his daddy's still. The ride also passes Windy Gap Vineyards, a bit of Bordeaux in the Brushies. The low elevations on this foothills route make it perfect for cool-weather riding. The start is just 40 minutes from Winston-Salem via four-lane U.S. 421.

IN DEPTH

This loop passes through an area that was once a hotbed of

illegal whiskey making. There's nothing to suggest it as you pedal along quiet Windy Gap Road today, but not so many years ago, these hills and hollows were infested with stills. Moonshiners combined sugar, corn mash, and water from small mountain streams to brew a clear concoction so potent it was almost pure alcohol. The country's largest seizure of illegal whiskey was made in Wilkes County. For years, the federal courthouse in Wilkesboro hosted a constant parade of moonshining cases.

Junior Johnson, the legendary NASCAR racer and team owner, learned how to drive on these back roads running whiskey for his father, a copper-still operator up Ingle Hollow. Junior perfected the "bootleg turn," an induced skid that forces a car into a 180-degree spin. He once got through a roadblock using a police siren and a red light in his grill. You'll pass Johnson's former racing shops at the foot of Ingle Hollow near the end of the ride.

The spirit of the future in these hills is wine, produced legally at several wineries in the Yadkin River Valley. At Windy Gap Vineyards, Allen and Sandra Hincher carefully tend the seven acres of premium grapes from which they make their award-winning wines. The vineyards and tasting room are a half-mile off the route on unpaved Pardue Farm Road, 24.5 miles into the ride. If you plan to visit the vineyards, you can begin and end the ride there. Check in with the Hinchers, park at the winery, ride the loop, and end your day with a tour of the facilities and a taste of some of Windy Gap's many varieties of wine.

The loop meanders along lightly traveled back roads through the rolling foothills and low mountains of Wilkes County. There's plenty of variety on the route. The mountains serve up a stout climb and a speedy descent, while the foothills offer flat stretches, short downhills, and equally brief climbs.

The mountainous leg of the route along Windy Gap Road is peaceful and picturesque. The road descends into a broad valley, where you'll pass several apple orchards and large fields that offer wide views of the surrounding mountains. The wooded rampart of hills rimming the valley is known locally as the Little Brushy Mountains. It's a low mountain range that protrudes 600 feet above the surrounding foothills. Several hundred cross-state riders enjoyed this scenic area during Cycle North Carolina 2000.

The ride's only tough spot begins about 12 miles in. A gradual climb leads to Windy Gap, a notch along the ridge top of the Little Brushies. You'll gain about 400 feet in elevation on this two-mile ascent. The elevation gain is modest by High Country standards, but two miles of climbing can get a little tedious nonetheless. The gap has an elevation of just 1,646 feet. Temperatures there are similar to those in the Piedmont, making this climb a comfortable alternative when Old Man Winter

Climbing past a lonely old farm on Hunting Creek Road

holds sway atop the Blue Ridge.

The descent from Windy Gap back into the foothills is short and fast. The smoothly paved road sheds 350 feet of elevation in just two-thirds of a mile. Once you cross the crest of the mountain, you'll be hurtling downhill at 40 miles per hour or more, but don't get cocky. A tight hairpin curve pops up suddenly, which will force you to slow down in a hurry. Use your brakes judiciously. Whatever you do, don't lock them, or you may find yourself inadvertently performing a bootleg turn of your own at the apex of this tricky curve.

The rest of the ride rolls along in typical foothills fashion through forests and farm country. Livestock outnumbers people here. You'll pass cattle, horses, and goats in the fields and untold thousands of chickens cooped up in low metal chicken houses. Mathis Mill Road is a classic country road lined with sturdy farmhouses, mighty oak trees, and old tobacco barns.

DIRECTIONS TO THE START

From U.S. 421 North, take Exit 272 (Clingman Road/Somers Road) and turn left at the stop sign at the end of the ramp; from U.S. 421 South, take the same exit and turn right at the end of the ramp. Drive approximately 1.4 miles to Temple Hill United Methodist Church. The ride starts from the community center and ball field located on the right across from the church.

If you prefer to begin the ride at Windy Gap Vineyards, take Exit 272 off U.S. 421 and follow the signs for 1.3 miles to the vineyards. Please ask permission before parking here.

Distance

26.8 miles

Challenge

✹✹ The two-mile climb up Windy Gap Road is the only long hill. The rest of the route features classic foothills riding, its flat stretches interspersed with short rises and descents.

Road Conditions and Cautions

The roads on the route are lightly traveled. The surfaces range from mirror smooth to grainy and uneven. The descent from Windy Gap has a steep 10 percent grade and a sudden sharp curve.

Cues

0.0   Turn **right** out of the parking area at the Temple Hill community center and ball field onto Somers Road (S.R. 2400).

4.6   Turn **right** at the crossroads onto Hunting Creek Road (S.R. 2412).

7.5   Turn **right** onto Jarvis Store Road (S.R. 2422).

8.3   Turn **left** at the stop sign at the old Jarvis Store onto

The "Little Brushies" wall this quiet valley.

Windy Gap Road (S.R. 2418); the green sign at the intersection says Mitchell Mill Road.

13.9   You'll reach Windy Gap, elevation 1,646 feet, the high point of the ride. Caution: A steep descent begins here.

15.3   Turn **right** onto Antioch Church Road (S.R. 2344).

17.5   Turn **right** at the stop sign onto Old 60 (S.R. 2318).

20.6   Turn **right** onto Mathis Mill Road (S.R. 2318).

23.9   Turn **right** onto Frog Level Road (S.R. 2317).

24.5   Windy Gap Vineyards is an optional side trip a half-mile off the route; turn **right** on unpaved Pardue Farm Road (S.R. 2316) if you wish to visit the winery.

24.8   Turn **right** at the stop sign onto Clingman Road (S.R. 2309).

25.7   Go **straight** at the stop sign across Wilkes/Yadkin Road (Old U.S. 421).

26.8   Turn **right** into the parking area for the Temple Hill community center and ball field to end the ride.

HIGHEST ELEVATION
1,646 feet on Windy Gap Road at Windy Gap, 13.9 miles into the ride

LOWEST ELEVATION
943 feet on Old 60 at River Creek, 19.6 miles into the ride

FOOD AND SERVICES
A country store is located on Somers Road a half-mile before the start of the ride. Redding's Country Kitchen Restaurant is off

Elevation Profile

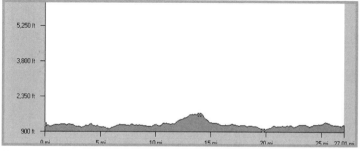

© 2002 DeLorme (www.delorme.com) *Topo USA* ® 4.0

the route on Wilkes/Yadkin Road (Old U.S. 421) east of the intersection with Somers Road.

ROADSIDE ATTRACTIONS

Windy Gap Vineyards is a small, family operation that produces several varieties of wine, including Cabernet Franc, Viognier, and Chardonnay. Free tastings and retail sales are available Thursday through Sunday or by appointment. The vineyards are located a half-mile off the route on unpaved Pardue Farm Road (S.R. 2316). For more information, call 336-984-3926 or visit www.ncwine.org.

Who needs bananas with all these apples?

A BITE OF THE BRUSHIES: THE APPLE COUNTRY LOOP

SHORT TAKE

You'll visit a sweet spot in the North Carolina foothills on this 34-mile loop ride. The route winds through the Brushy Mountains orchard country of Wilkes and Alexander Counties, combining climbs worthy of the Blue Ridge with elevations several thousand feet lower. Crisp air and crisp apples make this a great autumn ride.

IN DEPTH

Ready for a little temptation?

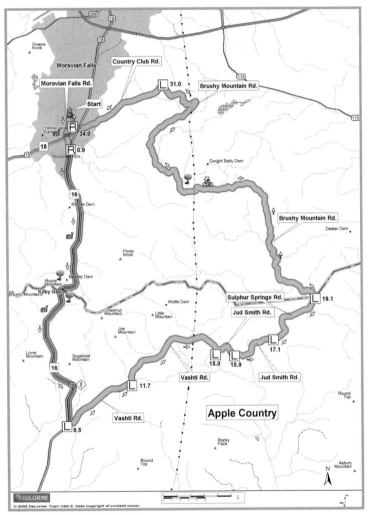

© 2002 DeLorme (www.delorme.com) *Topo USA* ® 4.0

"The luscious apples of Hesperides hang invitingly to tempt the palates of those who crave the rich, satisfying fruit of the gods," boasted an 1890s brochure touting the fruit of the Brushy Mountains. Today, the advertising pitch is a little subtler, but the apples, nectarines, peaches, and cherries grown here are just as tasty. The route passes through the Brushies' orchard belt twice as it loops through this low mountain range south of Wilkesboro.

The ride takes off from Moravian Falls, a small community a few miles north of "Apple Country." You wouldn't know it pedaling through this sleepy burg today, but a century ago, Moravian Falls was a major publishing center that produced nationally circulated papers with 50,000 and even 100,000 subscribers. The waterfall for which the town is named was discovered by a party of Moravian explorers 250 years ago. It's just off N.C. 18 on Falls Road.

It's an easy roll along N.C. 16 South toward "Apple Country." After a short initial rise, the road is flat for several miles. This is a good place to hook up in a paceline and blast down the highway's wide, smooth shoulder.

The wooded hills of the Brushy Mountains surround the level valley floor. The range runs parallel to the Blue Ridge but has peaks only half as high. Pore's Knob, the 2,680-foot high point, flanks N.C. 16 on the left. You'll see its rocky face looming behind Walnut Grove Baptist Church.

At the Brushy Mountain Service Station (where the only service is cold beer at the bar), the road begins a short climb into the Brushies. Apple orchards are spread throughout the hillsides. From the top of the climb back down, you'll pass at least five roadside apple houses, where, during the late summer

Orchard country atop Brushy Mountain

and fall, family orchardists ply their wares, surrounded by the seductive scent of fresh fruit.

The cluster of orchards atop these low mountains is no accident. The high spots of the Brushies are part of an isothermal belt that is perfect for growing fruit. While air temperature generally cools with elevation, cold air also sinks. The orchards in the Brushies occupy a sweet spot with regard to elevation—they're high enough to avoid the spring freezes in the valley but low enough not to be damaged by the cold, thinning air.

Once it exits N.C. 16 in northern Alexander County, the route leaves the orchard belt, roaming through the fields and forests of the foothills. The flat sections are punctuated by quick zips down to small creeks and short slogs back up. The rocky backside of the Brushies borders the road on the left during this speedy section of the ride.

The farther you ride from N.C. 16, the quieter the countryside gets. Eventually, you'll climb back into the mountains on Brushy Mountain Road. This quiet back road is framed by tall poplars as it runs for miles along Rocky Creek. The 800-

foot ascent, part of the annual Rides Around Wilkes (RAW) road-cycling event, has just a few steep spots. But since it's four miles long, the climb just goes on and on and on.

Toward the top of the ascent, the route loops back into the orchard belt. If you need a breather, you can pamper your palate at Parker's Produce Stand. Proprietor Gray Faw and his grandfather Jonah Parker can acquaint you with some tasty apples you won't find in your local supermarket. These friendly folks specialize in growing antique apple varieties like Magna Bonums and Brushy Mountain Limbertwigs. If your knowledge of apples ends at Red and Yellow Delicious, try some of these heirloom varieties and taste what you've been missing.

Once atop the mountain, the route winds past more orchards, some horse farms, and a big pumpkin patch. Then it's fun time, as Brushy Mountain Road twists down the mountain through two curvy descents. The second, longer plunge begins just past the Brushy Mountain General Store. It's a speedy slalom as the road sheds 730 feet over a 2.6-mile slide through the woods. A three-mile spin through suburban Wilkesboro returns you to the starting line in Moravian Falls.

DIRECTIONS TO THE START

From U.S. 421 in Wilkesboro, take the N.C. 16/N.C. 18 exit. Bear right at the top of the ramp onto N.C. 16/N.C. 18 and head south toward Taylorsville and Lenoir. Turn right at the second traffic signal onto Country Club Road (S.R. 2467), then turn right at the stop sign onto Moravian Falls Road (S.R. 1194). Leave your vehicle at Moravian Falls Optimist Club Park, located on the right just past the Pace service station.

DISTANCE

34.3 miles

CHALLENGE

✱✱The climb up the backside of the Brushies is long and has a couple of steep spots.

ROAD CONDITIONS AND CAUTIONS

N.C. 16 is moderately busy but has wide, smoothly paved shoulders for all but 1.4 miles of the route. All the other roads on the ride are lightly traveled and in good condition.

CUES

0.0   Turn **left** out of the parking lot at Moravian Falls Optimist Club Park onto Moravian Falls Road (S.R. 1194).

0.7   Go **straight** at the stop sign at N.C. 18.

0.9   Turn **right** at the stop sign onto N.C. 16 South.

5.2   You'll reach Kilby Gap, elevation 1,672 feet.

9.5   Turn **left** onto Vashti Road (S.R. 1403).

11.7   Turn **left** at the stop sign to continue on Vashti Road.

Parker's Produce Stand

15.0   Turn **left** onto Jud Smith Road (S.R. 1441).

15.9   Turn **left** at the bottom of the hill to continue on Jud Smith Road.

17.1   Turn **left** at the stop sign onto Sulphur Springs Road (S.R. 1001).

19.1   Turn **left** just before the bridge onto Brushy Mountain Road (S.R. 1001). A large road sign indicates that this is the turn to Wilkesboro.

26.0   You'll reach the top of the climb, elevation 2,195 feet.

31.0   Turn **left** onto Country Club Road (S.R. 2467) at the end of a long descent.

33.7   Go **straight** at the traffic signal at N.C. 16.

34.0   Turn **right** at the stop sign onto Moravian Falls Road.

34.3   The ride ends at Moravian Falls Optimist Club Park.

Elevation Profile

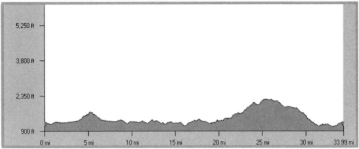

HIGHEST ELEVATION

2,195 feet on Brushy Mountain Road, 26 miles into the ride

LOWEST ELEVATION

1,056 feet on Country Club Road at Cub Creek, 33 miles into the ride

FOOD AND SERVICES

Country stores are located in Moravian Falls and atop the mountain, 28 miles into the ride. There is a small café in Moravian Falls.

ROADSIDE ATTRACTIONS

More than a half-dozen apple houses along the route offer apples, peaches, nectarines, cherries, and other locally grown produce. Look for peaches and nectarines in late summer and apples throughout the fall. Two of my favorite growers are Perry Lowe Orchards (336-921-3123), located on N.C. 16 just past Kilby Gap, and Parker's Orchard (336-921-3407), located near the top of the long climb.

Brushy Mountain General Store, located at 4973 Brushy Mountain Road, offers seasonal fruit, Amish baked goods, local crafts, wines, and cheeses. For more information, call 336-903-8501.

The Moravian Falls cascade is located just off the route in a privately owned park. Turn right onto N.C. 18 at the first stop sign on the route, then turn left onto Falls Road. The falls will be on your left at the bottom of the hill. For more information, call 336-667-6150.

All aboard—a paceline powers through the foothills.

THE HAPPY VALLEY TOUR

SHORT TAKE

You'll follow the trails of a pioneer, a patriot, and a legendary murder mystery on this half-century ride through the upper Yadkin River Valley. The ride passes through the historic and peaceful area known as Happy Valley. The rolling out-and-back route is a snap to follow and flat enough so everyone from novices to hard-core racers can have fun. It follows N.C. 268, a North Carolina Scenic Byway and part of the federally designated Overmountain Victory Trail. Featuring the lowest average elevation of any ride in the book, this tour makes a great cool-weather ride.

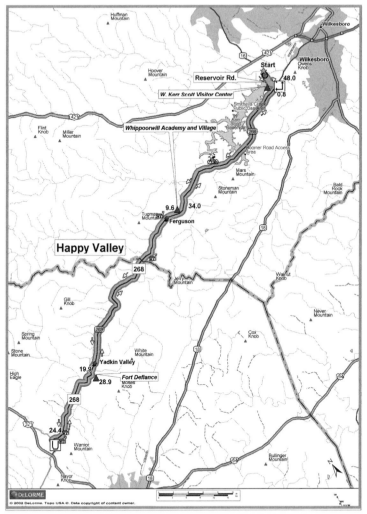

Huffman
Mountain

Wilkesboro

16 421

Wilkesboro
Owens
Knob

Hoover
Mountain

Reservoir Rd.

48.0

W. Kerr Scott Visitor Center

Start

0.8

Smithey's Creek
Public Use Area

Flint
Knob

421

Miller
Mountain

Whippoorwill Academy and Village

Scott

268

Boomer Road Access
Area

Bald
Rock
Mountain

Mars
Mountain

Stoneman
Mountain

9.6 **34.0**

Tugman
Mountain

Ferguson

18

Happy Valley

268

Jerry
Mountain

Walnut
Knob

Gill
Knob

Never
Mountain

Spring
Mountain

268

Cox
Knob

Stone
Mountain

White
Mountain

18

High
Eagle

19.9

Yadkin Valley

Fort Defiance

Moses
Knob

28.9

84

268

421

24.4

Warrior
Mountain

Bullinger
Mountain

84

Nayor
Knob

18

DeLORME

© 2002 DeLorme. Topo USA ®. Data copyright of content owner.

© 2002 DeLorme (www.delorme.com) *Topo USA* ® 4.0

In Depth

The ride begins and ends along the shores of W. Kerr Scott Reservoir. Severe floods in 1916 and 1940 ravaged the Yadkin River Valley, spurring the construction of this flood-control impoundment. Atop the dam, you'll enjoy a panoramic view of the lake on one side and the small towns of Wilkesboro and North Wilkesboro on the other.

As you pedal, you'll cross the lake and the Yadkin River several times. This fertile valley has played host to both the famous and the infamous.

The valley's most famous resident, Daniel Boone, didn't live here long. The wiry, wily woodsman took off for months, even years, at a stretch on hunting expeditions, leaving his family behind in a cramped cabin near Beaver Creek. Boone followed game up the buffalo trails into the high mountains while his wife, Rebecca, kept the home fires burning. The courageous pioneer, who blazed the Wilderness Trail to Kentucky, was something of a hunted man himself. Boone, said a Salisbury attorney, "had the honor of having more suits entered against him for debts than any other man of his day, chiefly small debts of five pounds and under, contracted for powder and shot."

A replica of Boone's Yadkin River Valley home stands at Whippoorwill Academy and Village, a living-history site that features a 19th-century schoolhouse, an old-time store, and an art gallery. Edith Carter, who founded the site, is a lifelong resident of the valley and has plenty of tales to tell.

The upper Yadkin River Valley was also home to the infamous Tom Dula, a Civil War veteran hanged in 1868 for the brutal murder of Laura Foster. Dula's trial attracted reporters from

Riders take a break at Whippoorwill Academy.

as far away as New York City. Did Dula kill his sweetheart? Or did femme fatale Ann Melton do the dastardly deed? The lurid story became a legend, spawning the folk song "Tom Dooley," which became a big hit for the Kingston Trio in the 1960s. Even today, Dula's guilt is a controversial topic in the valley; in 2002, Dula supporters petitioned North Carolina governor Mike Easley for a posthumous pardon. Dula is buried off the route near Ferguson. Laura Foster is buried in a grave surrounded by a whitewashed locust fence; it's visible in a field on the left about 16 miles into the ride.

The route snakes upstream along the Yadkin, eventually entering a long, broad valley. "This upper valley of the Yadkin is delightful," Professor Elisha Mitchell wrote in 1828. Today, Happy Valley possesses much the same charm it had when Mitchell visited it nearly two centuries ago. The gentle roll of the terrain, the wide views of the valley, and the scarcity of traffic make the valley a cyclist's delight.

Just off N.C. 268 is Fort Defiance, the 18th-century home of patriot leader William Lenoir. A self-educated man with broad civic interests, Lenoir led troops in the fight for American independence at the battle of Kings Mountain. In the fall of 1780, men assembled from several points in the mountains to converge at the battle site in upstate South Carolina. These men, disparaged as mongrels by the British, used their backwoods skills to defeat a contingent of loyalist troops in a battle that proved a turning point in the war. General Lenoir's restored home contains original furnishings, as well as relics of the Revolutionary War.

Located on the hill just past the Patterson School is the Chapel of Rest, a 1917 church open to visitors. The house of worship has a commanding view of the valley and the surrounding hills.

The ride turns around in Patterson, a small community with several cafés and community stores. The route up the valley isn't difficult, and the ride back is easier still. You'll experience some hilly moments on the return trip, but the route loses elevation overall on the trip back to the dam.

DIRECTIONS TO THE START

From U.S. 421, take Exit 286 (N.C. 268) in Wilkesboro. Go west on N.C. 268 approximately three miles to Reservoir Road. Turn right onto Reservoir Road. Park in the circle near the flagpole at the end of the dam. The ride leaves from Fish Dam Creek Overlook Park at W. Kerr Scott Dam and Reservoir.

DISTANCE

48.8 miles

CHALLENGE

✪♄ N.C. 268 offers rolling terrain and a few short, steep hills.

ROAD CONDITIONS AND CAUTIONS

N.C. 268 is popular with local riders. Prominent "Share the Road" signs alert motorists to the presence of cyclists. Some stretches in the upper valley are curvy and offer limited sight distance. Traffic is moderate to light.

CUES

0.0	Go **straight** across the dam on Reservoir Road toward N.C. 268.
0.8	Turn **right** at the stop sign onto N.C. 268 West.
9.6	You'll reach Whippoorwill Academy and Village, located on the right just off the route.
19.9	You'll reach Fort Defiance, located to your left just off the route.
24.4	**Turn around** at the stop sign in Patterson just past Valley Foods.
48.0	Turn **left** on Reservoir Road to return to the starting

Elevation Profile

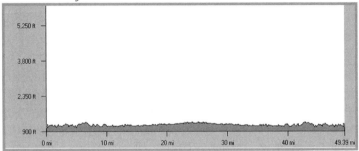

© 2002 DeLorme (www.delorme.com) *Topo USA* ® 4.0

point; look for the large brown sign for W. Kerr Scott Dam and Reservoir.

48.8   You'll end the ride at Fish Dam Creek Overlook Park.

HIGHEST ELEVATION

1,361 feet at the turnaround point near Patterson, 24.4 miles into the ride

LOWEST ELEVATION

1,034 feet at the bridge over W. Kerr Scott Reservoir near the Blood Creek Overlook, 4.7 miles and 44.1 miles into the ride

FOOD AND SERVICES

Water and restrooms are available at the W. Kerr Scott Dam

and Reservoir Visitor Center near the start and finish. You'll find country stores at regular intervals along the route. Two small cafés are located in Patterson near the halfway point of the ride.

ROADSIDE ATTRACTIONS

Whippoorwill Academy and Village, located in Ferguson, features an old-time school, a store, a chapel, and a replica of Daniel Boone's Yadkin River Valley cabin. The Tom Dooley Art Museum houses Dula's tombstone and war records, a lock of Laura Foster's hair, and paintings by Edith F. Carter on Dula's life. Whippoorwill is open on a limited basis Saturday and Sunday afternoons and at other times by appointment. For more information, call 336-973-3237 or visit www.wilkesnc.org/history/whippoorwill.

Fort Defiance, located in Patterson, offers tours of General William Lenoir's home, built in 1790. The site hosts a Revolutionary War encampment the last Saturday in September. For more information, call 828-758-1671.

Fort Defiance, home to patriot William Lenoir

The W. Kerr Scott Dam and Reservoir Visitor Center, located in Wilkesboro near the start and finish, offers exhibits, a short film on the construction of the dam, and restrooms. For more information, call 336-921-3390 or visit www.wilkesnc.org/history/wkerr.htm.

OUTDOOR OPTIONS

W. Kerr Scott Reservoir offers opportunities for boating, fishing, and camping. This United States Army Corps of Engineers facility has several mountain-biking trails under development, including the Dark Mountain Trail, located near the start and finish. For more information, call 336-921-3390 or visit http://www.wilkesnc.org/history/wkerr.htm.

WEST AND SOUTHWEST OF BOONE

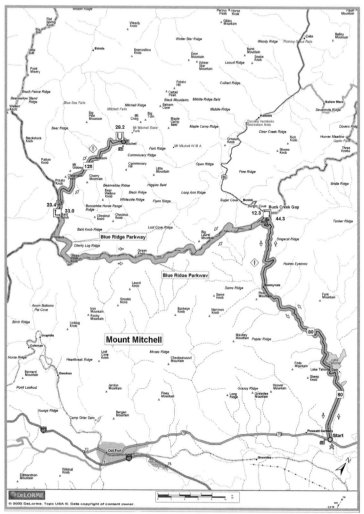

© 2002 DeLorme (www.delorme.com) *Topo USA* ® 4.0

Fir trees frame the Parkway near N.C. 128.

THE MOUNT MITCHELL CLIMB

SHORT TAKE

This epic 56-mile out-and-back ride soars to the top of the highest mountain in eastern America. It's 28 miles of almost pure hill from Marion, North Carolina, in the foothills to the end of the road near Mount Mitchell's peak. The pain is obvious, but the rewards include sweeping views and several long, screaming descents on the return.

IN DEPTH

Gravity is not your friend during much of this grinding, grueling ride into the sky. A full mile of elevation change and nearly 11,000 feet of climbing overall combine to make this route extremely challenging.

Beyond the pure rigors of the climb, you must be prepared for wild swings in the weather. Given the 5,200-foot gain in altitude, it can be up to 30 degrees cooler atop Mount Mitchell than in the foothills. And if the chill isn't enough, you may also get wet. Mount Mitchell is a precipitation magnet. The massive Black Mountains wring out moist air as clouds rise over the range. The rainfall totals here are worthy of the Pacific Northwest.

A logistical problem with this route is its lack of stores and public water sources. A restaurant and snack bar await at the state park atop Mount Mitchell, but there are no places to rehydrate or refuel between the lower reaches of the valley and the peak. Two water bottles may not cut it on a hot, muggy day.

Though this stout ride requires special planning, it isn't one big grimace. It begins pleasantly with a warmup along Buck Creek on the valley floor. The route winds around scenic Lake Tahoma, then finds the creek again. The creek is a constant companion as N.C. 80 climbs from the foothills to the top of the Blue Ridge at Buck Creek Gap. The road follows Buck Creek almost to its source through several dozen hairpin curves surrounded by a dense oak-hickory forest that is green and shady in summertime and ablaze with color in the fall. Tour DuPont riders flew down this route in 1994 and climbed it in 1995.

At unmarked Buck Creek Gap (elevation 3,344 feet), the ride enters the Blue Ridge Parkway. You're out of the deep forest now, riding along the edge of a bold ridge that offers soaring views of the foothills below. An opening climb on the park-

*Curvy N.C. 80
twists toward Buck
Creek Gap.*

way gives way to a lengthy descent. Unfortunately, every inch
of it must be tediously reclaimed on the way to the top. Thanks
to its three tunnels, its numerous scenic overlooks, and its thick
stands of pink-blooming rosebay rhododendron, this stretch of
the parkway offers plenty of distractions from the pain of the
climb.

Mount Mitchell is visible from several overlooks on the right
side of the parkway. Though Mitchell is the East's highest peak,
it's not distinctive. It's merely the highest bump on a long ridge
of tall mountains—the Black Mountain range. The Black Mountains really do look black, a result of their spruce-fir forests and
the clouds that cluster along their shadowy peaks.

At "the Pinnacle" (Milepost 354), the Blue Ridge is deserted
by its namesake parkway, which heads toward the Black Mountains. The route soon turns onto N.C. 128, a steep, winding
road that climbs nearly 1,500 feet over 4.8 miles as it skirts
Clingman's Peak on the way to Mount Mitchell. The ride's
toughest climbing starts here.

You're grinding up a mountain that claimed the man for

whom it is named. The East's highest peak honors the memory of Dr. Elisha Mitchell, a University of North Carolina science professor who fell to his death on an exploration of the Black Mountains in 1857. Mitchell had visited the Blacks several times before and was engaged in a scholarly debate with Thomas Clingman as to who had first measured the highest peak in the Appalachian range. In the Blacks in 1857 to take new measurements that he hoped would solidify his claim as the discoverer of the highest peak, Mitchell slipped and fell to his death not far from the mountain that today bears his name. The body was recovered by Tom Wilson, a local man who had been Mitchell's guide on his earlier forays in the Blacks; the mountain known as Big Tom acknowledges Wilson's role. Clingman, Mitchell's rival, was assigned a lower peak; lofty Clingmans Dome in the Smokies is also named for him.

Atop the Blacks, it feels like Canada. It looks like it, too. You'd expect to find the mountains' spruce-fir forests 1,000 miles north. Though they've survived since the last ice age, the forests are now ghostly, many dead trees mixed in among the living. Acid rain and a tiny insect predator, the balsam woolly adelgid, are twin scourges laying waste to this rare and fragile ecosystem.

Just getting to the top is an accomplishment to be savored. This may not be the time to think about how riders like George Hincapie can do the 100 miles from Spartanburg, South Carolina, to the top of Mount Mitchell in five hours. The annual Assault on Mount Mitchell ride in May brings lesser riders to tears.

After a well-deserved break at the top of the mountain, it's time to turn around. What went up (slowly) must now come down (quickly). The descents on this ride are exhilarating. N.C. 128 is smooth and swooping, offering broad vistas on the way from Mount Mitchell to the parkway. On N.C. 80, you'll soar down a succession of switchbacks from the top of the ridge into the valley below. Tuck in, lean, carve the turns, and remember that, yes, gravity is your friend again.

DIRECTIONS TO THE START

From Interstate 40, take Exit 85 and go north on U.S. 221 to U.S. 70. Turn left onto U.S. 70 West and proceed approximately two miles to the junction with N.C. 80 in Pleasant Gardens, located near Marion. A store and the large Tom Johnson Camping Center are near this intersection. Always ask for permission before parking in any private lot.

DISTANCE

56.4 miles

CHALLENGE

✪✪✪ No ride in this book has more climbing.

ROAD CONDITIONS AND CAUTIONS

N.C. 80 is in decent condition, but watch for some wavy irregularities in the road surface, which could pose a problem at high speed as you descend from Buck Creek Gap. Exercise caution on the descents. The Blue Ridge Parkway and N.C. 128

are in good condition. Front and rear reflectors or lamps are required for the three tunnels on the Blue Ridge Parkway. Parkway regulations require cyclists to ride single file.

Cues

0.0	Follow N.C. 80 North toward Mount Mitchell.
12.3	Turn **left** onto the Blue Ridge Parkway access ramp at Buck Creek Gap, then **left** at the stop sign onto the parkway heading south.
23.4	Turn **right** onto N.C. 128 and head toward Mount Mitchell.
28.2	**Turn around** at the parking lot near the summit of Mount Mitchell.
33.0	Turn **left** at the stop sign and head north on the Blue Ridge Parkway.
44.3	Turn **right** onto the N.C. 80 access ramp, then **right** at the stop sign onto N.C. 80 heading toward Marion.
56.4	You'll return to the junction of N.C. 80 and U.S. 70.

Elevation Profile

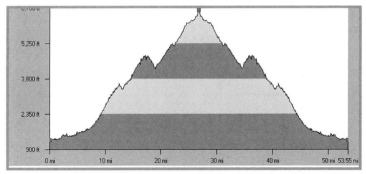

© 2002 DeLorme (www.delorme.com) *Topo USA ®* 4.0

HIGHEST ELEVATION

6,628 feet in the parking lot near the summit of Mount Mitchell, 28.2 miles into the ride

LOWEST ELEVATION

1,277 feet along Buck Creek near the start and finish

FOOD AND SERVICES

Mount Mitchell State Park has a snack bar and restroom facilities near the summit of the mountain and a restaurant just off N.C. 128. The only other stores are associated with private campgrounds off N.C. 80 along Buck Creek. These stores come too soon in the ride to be helpful. Make sure you carry adequate food and drink.

*Summer wildflowers
are everywhere.*

OUTDOOR OPTIONS

Mount Mitchell State Park offers camping facilities and miles of hiking trails. For more information, call 828-675-4611 or visit www.ils.unc.edu/parkproject/visit/momi/home.html.

N.C. 261 near Bakersville

A CLIMB TO CLOUDLAND: THE ROAN MOUNTAIN TOUR

SHORT TAKE

You'll climb into the clouds on this two-state loop ride to Roan Mountain, one of the most ecologically diverse areas in the southern Appalachians. This metric-century route begins and ends with descents, but don't be fooled. It's plenty steep, boasting two major climbs and 8,600 feet of climbing overall. Rushing creeks, tall mountain ridges, and broad pastures provide inspiration; steep, switchback-loaded ascents provoke perspiration; and the swooping downhill from Carver's Gap to the finish promotes exhilaration.

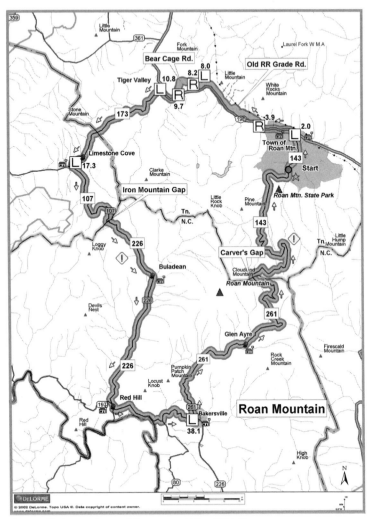

© 2002 DeLorme (www.delorme.com) *Topo USA* ® 4.0

In Depth

The route begins with a pleasant side trip down Old Railroad Grade Road in the state of Tennessee. This glide of a ride follows the bed of the old East Tennessee and Western North Carolina Railroad (the "Tweetsie" line) as it rolls along the Doe River. You're on a public road, but the scenery and the narrow roadbed make it feel like a rail trail, albeit a very smoothly paved one. If you had a long driveway to your fantasy mountain estate, it might look like this.

After a few twists and turns, the route reenters U.S. 19E for a short stretch, then turns left onto Tenn. 173 to follow Simmerly Creek. You'll pedal through a sparsely populated area of fields and forests that opens to wider views at the community of Limestone Cove.

If you need food or fluids, visit the store on Tenn. 107 that's just off the route near the junction with Tenn. 173. Once you begin Tenn. 107, you're on the first of the route's two classic climbs.

Mountain climbs seem to follow a pattern reminiscent of a scene from an old Warner Brothers cartoon. Bugs Bunny has been conned into a big cauldron, thinking it's a bathtub. As he washes, he sniffs and says, "Something smells delicious, Doc. Whatcha cookin'?" "Wabbit," Elmer replies, at which time Bugs realizes he's in the soup.

Both of this ride's major climbs begin just as innocently as you ride along a wide, bold creek. "This isn't so bad," you'll think. Then, gradually, the creek gets louder and the road steeper. Soon, the creek, still audible as it rushes over rocks, isn't visible at all, swallowed by the summer wildflowers and

Farmland framed by high hills

brush at its bank. The road departs the creek to begin turning back and forth as it scales the ridge. At the end of each bend, you'll anticipate seeing sky through the trees, a sure sign the top is near. That hope will be dashed over and over again. Yes, you're in hot water now.

Though the climb to Iron Mountain Gap at the state line lifts you to an elevation of 3,710 feet, you've gained only about 1,300 feet since the flats at Limestone Cove. The climb back into Tennessee up Roan Mountain has a net gain of over 3,000 feet! It's important to pace yourself on a ride of this length and difficulty and not give too much too soon.

The ride cruises downhill into North Carolina. At the small community of Buladean, it flattens and the forest opens to reveal views of the Roan Mountain massif to your left. The route rolls through the small communities of Red Hill and Loafers Glory as it winds toward the Mitchell County seat of Bakersville.

Bakersville (elevation 2,500 feet) is a sleepy, two-stoplight town at the foot of the day's second major climb, the grind back to the state line at Roan Mountain. The route turns left onto N.C. 261. A right at the same intersection will take you toward a convenience store with a nice park and greenway across the street; it's a good idea to rest here in the relative warmth of the valley, as it'll be a good 15 degrees cooler at Carver's Gap.

You'll begin climbing shortly after leaving Bakersville on N.C. 261. It's a strain just getting to the top of unmarked Pumpkin Patch Gap, the first big hill out of town; the misery is compounded by the knowledge that every foot climbed here will be given back on a descent, then reclaimed as the route follows Little Rock Creek toward its source in the mountains high above.

The scenery provides a distraction from the pain of the climb. The wide views through the valley reveal the balds and rock outcrops at the mountaintop. Bold branches rush over rocks to spill into Little Rock Creek, the main stream. As the road climbs to the top, the landscape changes. The classic oak-hickory forest so prevalent in the southern Appalachians gives way to woods dominated by beeches and maples. Beyond that, yellow birches and buckeyes, stunted by the wind and weather, hold on. High atop Roan, spruces and firs—species first pushed south eons ago during a period of glaciation—hold sway. If the trip from Bakersville to Roan seems arduous, it should—it's the biological equivalent of a 1,000-mile drive north to Ontario, Canada.

At an elevation of 5,512 feet, Carver's Gap is the high point of the ride. You're not atop Roan Mountain at this point, but rather in a notch that separates Roan (on the left) from Jane Bald (on the right). A two-mile spur road to the left ascends to the top of Roan; an admission fee is charged.

Two distinct ecosystems collide at this very spot. On your

left, the massive mountain hosts a relic spruce-fir forest and a 600-acre garden of purple rhododendron. On your right is a grassy bald with barely a tree in sight, the first of a string of balds that extends for miles. "It is the most beautiful of all the high mountains," Dr. Elisha Mitchell wrote of his journey to the area in 1836. "The top of the Roan may be described as a vast meadow without a tree to obstruct this prospect, where a person may gallop his horse for a mile or two with Carolina at his feet on one side and Tennessee on the other, and a green ocean of mountains rising in tremendous billows immediately around him."

And speaking of billows, don't be surprised if a sunny day turns cloudy here. Moist air tends to condense as it rises over the ridge. The inn that once graced the mountaintop at Roan was named the Cloudland Hotel for good reason.

Your exhaustion will be relieved by an adrenalin rush on the outstanding descent from Carver's Gap back to the Doe River Valley. You'll encounter a few tight curves, but nothing too tricky. The road is smooth. You can use the entire lane without having to worry too much about potholes, patches, and gravel. The expansive views at the top soon give way to a screaming ride through a hardwood forest that's a green blur in the summertime.

DIRECTIONS TO THE START

From Banner Elk, North Carolina, go south on N.C. 194 for seven miles to U.S. 19E. Turn right onto U.S. 19E and drive seven miles north to the town of Roan Mountain, Tennessee. Turn left onto Tenn. 143 North and travel two miles to the visitor center at Roan Mountain State Park. You can leave your vehicle in the lot at the visitor center.

DISTANCE

61.4 miles

CHALLENGE

⊗⊗⊗ The distance and the two major climbs make this ride truly tough.

ROAD CONDITIONS AND CAUTIONS

U.S. 19E near the start of the ride is busy, but the generous, smooth shoulders make it easy to avoid traffic. Caution is required on the ride's two long descents from the state line. N.C. 226 from Red Hill through Bakersville is narrow and busy. It's difficult for vehicles to pass cyclists in this stretch, so be prepared to pull into a driveway to let folks get by.

You'll climb through several types of forest on the way to Carver's Gap.

CUES

0.0   Turn **right** out of the visitor center at Roan Mountain State Park onto Tenn. 143 South.

2.0   Turn **left** at the stop sign onto U.S. 19E North.

3.9   Turn **right** onto Old Railroad Grade Road.

8.0   Turn **left** onto unmarked Hershel Julian Road. If you get to the iron bridge on Old Railroad Grade Road, you've gone too far.

8.2   Turn **right** at the stop sign after the bridge over the Doe River onto unmarked Bear Cage Road.

9.7   Turn **right** at the stop sign onto U.S. 19E North.

10.8   Turn **left** onto Tenn. 173 (Simmerly Creek Road) at Tiger Valley.

17.3   Turn **left** at the stop sign onto Tenn. 107 East in the Limestone Cove community.

21.9   You'll reach the Tennessee-North Carolina line at Iron Mountain Gap, elevation 3,710 feet. Tenn. 107 becomes N.C. 226. A long descent begins here.

38.1 Turn **left** onto N.C. 261 North (Crimson Laurel Way) in Bakersville.

50.8 You'll reach the state line at Carver's Gap, elevation 5,512 feet. N.C. 261 becomes Tenn. 143. A long descent begins here.

61.4 You'll end the ride at the visitor center at Roan Mountain State Park.

HIGHEST ELEVATION

5,512 feet at Carver's Gap, 50.8 miles into the ride

LOWEST ELEVATION

2,060 feet at the junction of U.S. 19E and Tenn. 173 at Tiger Valley, 10.8 miles into the ride

Elevation Profile

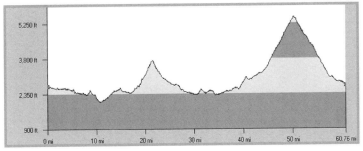

© 2002 DeLorme (www.delorme.com) *Topo USA* ® 4.0

FOOD AND SERVICES

Restrooms are available at the visitor center at Roan Mountain State Park. You can purchase food at several convenience stores and restaurants in the town of Roan Mountain, Tennessee. The stores at Limestone Cove in Tennessee and the North Carolina communities of Buladean, Red Hill, Bakersville, and Glen Ayre are spaced six to eight miles apart.

OUTDOOR OPTIONS

The Appalachian Trail crosses the route at Iron Mountain Gap and Carver's Gap. The AT and other foot trails in the Roan Mountain area traverse lush evergreen forests and sweeping balds. None of these trails is open to bicycles.

Roan Mountain State Park is a complete resort offering hiking, camping, cabin rentals, fishing, and swimming. For more information, call 800-250-8620 or visit www.state.tn.us/environment/parks/roanmtn.

Field and forest on Bear Cage Road

THE TWEETSIE TRAIL

SHORT TAKE

You'll trace the tracks of the real Tweetsie Railroad on this easy 19-mile out-and-back route. You'll roll along the rushing Doe River on an old railroad bed transformed into a smooth country lane. The ride begins and ends at Roan Mountain State Park, a beautiful Tennessee resort with plenty to see and do.

IN DEPTH

Mention Tweetsie Railroad and most folks think of the amusement park between Boone and Blowing Rock in North Carolina, where Old West lawmen defend a lumbering old steam

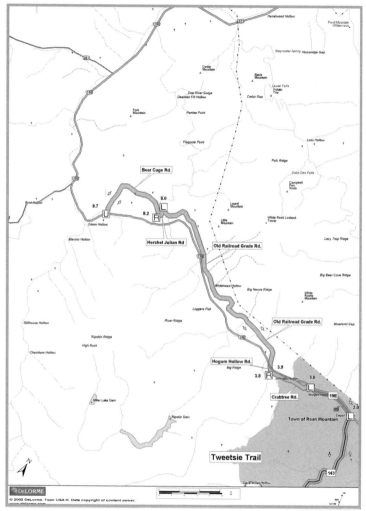

© 2002 DeLorme (www.delorme.com) *Topo USA* ® 4.0

Tight squeeze—a rider slips past solid rock on the Old Railroad Grade Road.

train from a comical crew of bad guys. Few people realize that the coal-fired locomotive making lazy circles around the theme park was once part of a real railroad line that played a pivotal role in the history of the High Country.

That proud old locomotive was one of 13 that once ran on the East Tennessee and Western North Carolina line, a narrow-gauge railroad built around 1880 to connect Johnson City, Tennessee, to iron mines near Cranberry, North Carolina. The line, eventually extended to Boone, opened the rugged and isolated region to trade and tourism.

The jaunty little train with the bold red-and-gold smoke-stack hauled timber and iron ore out of the mountains. It also picked up passengers. Roan Mountain was a popular picnic spot.

If you wanted to hop the train there, you had to flag it down and run to catch it.

Virtually no one knew the ET & WNC line by its given name. Some mountain wags called it the "Eat Taters and Wear No Clothes" route. To most folks, though, the train was simply "Tweetsie."

A devastating flood in 1940 wiped out the upper part of the line. The rest was abandoned in 1950, much to the chagrin of many mountain people, who loved the train and its shrill steam whistle. A local schoolgirl wrote a verse lamenting Tweetsie's passing: "Our memory of her is clear and plain. / Please send us back our little train."

Not everyone loved the railroad, though. A woman along the line complained after the train ran over one of her pigs. When the railroad company was slow to pay, she greased the tracks with the lard of the hapless pig, derailing the train. The company promptly paid up.

This route runs along the old railroad grade for about eight miles. The narrow roadway resembles a smoothly paved driveway more than a public road. At several points, it squeezes through narrow slits blasted through large rocks. The Doe River, fringed with rhododendron and tall hemlocks, rushes below. A canopy of tall hardwoods covers the hillsides. The road has plenty of pull-offs with well-worn trails leading to the banks of the rushing river. The rail bed is fairly flat, but the surrounding terrain is steep. I remember riding through as an old man was digging potatoes in his garden. One of the taters rolled out of his garden, down the bank, and across the road before he could catch it.

The route alternates between wooded stretches that seem

like wilderness and sections where you're riding just a few feet from folks' front doors. The narrow roadbed and the dearth of vehicles make it easy to imagine that you're rolling down a railway.

The ride begins and ends at Roan Mountain State Park, a resort that offers cabins, camping, and a wealth of recreational activities. You can picnic, hike, fish, play tennis, and splash around in the heated pool or the cool, crystal-clear Doe River. Roan Mountain's rhododendron gardens and the largest grassy balds in the Appalachians are about eight miles past the park on Tenn. 143.

Because the ride is an out-and-back, it can be as long or as short as you like. Cyclists uncomfortable with traffic can skip

Doe River from the bridge on Hershel Julian Road

the first four miles and begin on Old Railroad Grade Road. If steep hills are a problem, skip the last mile of Bear Cage Road, which contains the ride's only grinding grade. No matter how far you ride, the return trip will be a gentle ascent.

The route for "The Tweetsie Trail" is part of the Tennessee Department of Transportation's official bicycle-route system. Many of the turns are marked with prominent green bike-route signs to help you stay on track. One that's not well marked is the left turn from Old Railroad Grade Road onto Hershel Julian Road. If you miss it, you'll soon come to an old iron bridge over the Doe River, itself a worthy destination. Just turn around at the bridge to rejoin the route.

DIRECTIONS TO THE START

From Banner Elk, North Carolina, go south on N.C. 194 for seven miles to U.S. 19E. Turn right onto U.S. 19E and drive seven miles north to the town of Roan Mountain, Tennessee. Turn left onto Tenn. 143 North and travel two miles to the visitor center at Roan Mountain State Park, where the ride begins.

DISTANCE

19.4 miles

CHALLENGE

✷ The ride's only tough spot is a steep hill on Bear Cage Road that's less than a quarter-mile long. The return trip is a gentle uphill grade.

Road Conditions and Cautions

Tenn. 143 between Roan Mountain State Park and U.S. 19E is smooth surfaced; it has wide shoulders near the town of Roan Mountain. The one-mile leg on U.S. 19E near the start of the ride is busy, but the generous, smooth-surfaced shoulders make it easy to avoid traffic. The other roads on the route are smooth, narrow country lanes with little traffic.

Cues

0.0   Turn **right** out of the visitor center at Roan Mountain State Park onto Tenn. 143 South.

2.0   Turn **left** at the stop sign onto U.S. 19E North.

3.0   Turn **left** onto Crabtree Road.

3.8   Turn **right** onto Hogum Hollow Road.

3.9   Turn **left** at the stop sign onto U.S. 19E, then make a **quick right** onto Old Railroad Grade Road.

8.0   Turn **left** onto unmarked Hershel Julian Road. If you get to the iron bridge on Old Railroad Grade Road, you've gone too far.

8.2   Turn **right** at the stop sign after the bridge over the Doe River onto unmarked Bear Cage Road.

8.7   You'll crest a big hill.

9.7   **Turn around** at the stop sign at U.S. 19E.

10.7   You'll crest a big hill.

11.2   Turn **left** onto Hershel Julian Road at the Doe River bridge.

11.4   Turn **right** at the stop sign onto unmarked Old Railroad Grade Road.

15.5   Turn **left** at the stop sign onto U.S. 19E South, then make a **quick right** onto Hogum Hollow Road.

15.6   Turn **left** just past the Doe River bridge onto Crabtree Road.

16.4   Turn **right** at the stop sign onto U.S. 19E South.

17.4   Turn **right** onto Tenn. 143 and ride north toward Carver's Gap.

19.4   Turn **left** into the visitor center at Roan Mountain State Park to end the ride.

Elevation Profile

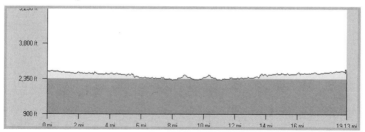

© 2002 DeLorme (www.delorme.com) *Topo USA* ® 4.0

HIGHEST ELEVATION

2,676 feet on Tenn. 143 near the start and finish

LOWEST ELEVATION

2,303 feet on Hershel Julian Road at the Doe River bridge, eight miles and 11.2 miles into the ride

FOOD AND SERVICES

Restrooms are available at the visitor center at Roan Mountain State Park. Food may be purchased at several convenience stores and restaurants in the town of Roan Mountain.

ROADSIDE ATTRACTIONS

The visitor center at Roan Mountain State Park offers information on the park and the surrounding area. The Peg Leg

Iron Ore Mine is on the site. The park's Dave Miller Homestead is a turn-of-the-20th-century mountain farm; it's north of the visitor center off Tenn. 143. For more information, call 800-250-8620 or visit www.state.tn.us/environment/parks/roanmtn.

OUTDOOR OPTIONS

Roan Mountain State Park is a 2,000-acre resort that offers hiking, camping, cabins, fishing, and swimming. For more information, call 800-250-8620 or visit www.state.tn.us/environment/parks/roanmtn.

APPENDIX A RIDE LIST IN ORDER OF CHALLENGE

Ride	Length	Challenge	Min.Elev.	Max.Elev.	Max.-Min.	Start/Finish
Railroad Grade Road	20.4	½	2,859	2,984	125	Fleetwood
Tweetsie Trail	19.4	1	2,303	2,676	373	Roan Mountain, Tenn.
Shady Valley	11.9	1	2,661	3,038	377	Shady Valley, Tenn.
Cove Creek	14.4	1	2,700	3,288	588	Sugar Grove
Happy Valley	48.8	1½	1,034	1,361	327	W. Kerr Scott Dam
Blowing Rock	11.5	1½	3,444	3,995	551	Blowing Rock
Fiddler's Run	25	1½	2,465	3,027	562	Cumberland Knob
Tour de Frescoes	23.3	2	2,715	3,248	533	Glendale Springs
Shatley Springs	32	2	2,548	3,172	624	Shatley Springs
Moonshine and Wine	26.8	2	943	1,646	703	Temple Hill ball field
Glade Valley	33.2	2	2,530	3,288	758	Cumberland Knob
Trade Tour	44.6	2	2,700	3,511	811	Sugar Grove
Lump Loop	25.2	2	2,843	3,713	870	Cascades Park

Ride	Length	Challenge	Min.Elev.	Max.Elev.	Max.-Min.	Start/Finish
Boone Back Roads	24	2	3,105	3,995	890	Boone
Doughton Park	36	2	2,709	3,744	1,035	Milepost 230
Bulldog's Bite	32.1	2	2,670	3,746	1,076	Valle Crucis
Apple Country	34.3	2	1,056	2,195	1,139	Moravian Falls
Grandfather Mountain	21.4	2	3,380	4,535	1,155	Julian Price Park
Buffalo Trail	37.1	2½	2,782	3,724	942	Island Park, Todd
Snake Mountain	42.5	2½	2,864	4,479	1,615	Island Park, Todd
Beech Ball	38.2	2½	2,508	4,135	1,627	Valle Crucis
Valle Crucis	46.8	2½	2,670	4,333	1,663	Valle Crucis
Road to Damascus	37.7	2½	1,905	3,694	1,789	Damascus, Va.
Beech Mountain	22.4	2½	2,670	5,085	2,415	Valle Crucis
Roan Mountain	61.4	3	2,060	5,512	3,452	Roan Mountain, Tenn.
Mount Mitchell	56.4	3	1,277	6,628	5,351	Marion

APPENDIX B
FOR MORE INFORMATION

Visitor Information

Alexander County Chamber of Commerce
104 West Main Avenue
Taylorsville, N.C. 28681
828-632-8141
www.alexandercountychamber.com

Alleghany County Chamber of Commerce
P.O. Box 1237
Sparta, N.C. 28675
800-372-5473
www.sparta-nc.com

Ashe Chamber of Commerce and Visitors Center
6 North Jefferson Avenue
West Jefferson, N.C. 28694
336-246-9550
www.ashechamber.com

Avery/Banner Elk Chamber of Commerce
P.O. Box 335
Banner Elk, N.C. 28604
800-972-2183
www.banner-elk.com

Beech Mountain Chamber of Commerce
403-A Beech Mountain Parkway
Beech Mountain, N.C. 28604
828-387-9283
www.beechmtn.com

Blowing Rock Chamber of Commerce
P.O. Box 406
Blowing Rock, N.C. 28605
800-295-7851
www.blowingrock.com

Blue Ridge Parkway Association, Inc.
P.O. Box 2136
Asheville, N.C. 28802
www.blueridgeparkway.org

This association publishes a comprehensive, free Blue Ridge Parkway guide and posts a mile-by-mile guide to parkway attractions on its website.

Blue Ridge Travel Association of Virginia
731 Factory Outlet Drive, Suite D-8
Max Meadows, Va. 24360
800-446-9670
www.virginiablueridge.org

This regional travel bureau provides information on lodgings, attractions, and events in the mountains of southwestern Virginia.

Boone Area Chamber of Commerce
208 Howard Street
Boone, N.C. 28607
888-251-9867
www.visitboonenc.com

Caldwell County Chamber of Commerce
1909 Hickory Boulevard S.E.
Lenoir, N.C. 28645
828-726-0616
www.caldwellcochamber.org

Elizabethton Chamber of Commerce
P.O. Box 190
Elizabethton, Tenn. 37644
423-547-3850
www.tourelizabethton.com

Galax-Carroll-Grayson Chamber of Commerce
405 Main Street
Galax, Va. 24333
276-236-2184
www.gcgchamber.com

High Country Host
1700 Blowing Rock Road
Boone, N.C. 28607
800-438-7500
www.highcountryhost.com
   This regional travel bureau provides information on lodgings,

attractions, and events in a six-county area of northwestern North Carolina. Its website has extensive Blue Ridge Parkway information.

Johnson County Chamber of Commerce
P.O. Box 1
Mountain City, Tenn. 37683
423-727-5800
www.johnsoncountychamber.org

Mitchell County Chamber of Commerce
79 Parkway Road
Spruce Pine, N.C. 28777
800-227-3912
www.mitchell-county.com

North Carolina Department of Commerce
Division of Tourism, Film, and Sports Development
301 North Wilmington Street
Raleigh, N.C. 27601
800-VISIT NC
www.visitnc.com

This source offers North Carolina travel information, including state highway maps, travel guides, and events calendars.

Washington County Chamber of Commerce
179 East Main Street
Abingdon, Va. 24210
276-628-8141
www.washingtonvachamber.org

Wilkes County Chamber of Commerce
P.O. Box 727
North Wilkesboro, N.C. 28659
336-838-8662
www.wilkesnc.org

Cycling-Specific Information

Damascus, Virginia, Mountain Bike Pages
www.bikeguy.net

Tom Horsch's website has everything you'll want to know about road and mountain biking in the Damascus area.

NCDOT Division of Bicycle and Pedestrian Transportation
1552 Mail Service Center
Raleigh, N.C. 27699-1552
919-733-2804
www.ncdot.org/transit/bicycle

NCDOT offers information on cycling regulations and statewide listings of bicycle shops, events, and clubs. Its website has a link for ordering state cycling maps.

Rocket Man's Climb Ratings
www.ncbikeclub.org/documents/
Rocket_Man_Climb_Ratings.htm

This website's controversial ratings of western North Carolina climbs are posted by a member of the Raleigh-area North Carolina Bike Club.

Techniques for Planning Bicycle Trips
on the Blue Ridge Parkway
www.nukefix.org/parkway/

This website offers mind-numbing detail on every climb on the Blue Ridge Parkway.

Training Ideas for Flatlander Cyclists Trying to Climb Hills
http://greenvillespinners.com/articles/flatlander.html

This website has serious and tongue-in-cheek training tips.

Weather Information

National Weather Service Forecast Office, Blacksburg, Virginia
www.erh.noaa.gov/er/rnk/

This website offers text and graphical forecasts for parts of the High Country, including Alleghany, Ashe, Watauga, and Wilkes Counties in North Carolina and Grayson and Carroll Counties in Virginia. The graphical forecasts include temperature, wind, and precipitation predictions for three-hour intervals.

National Weather Service Forecast Office, Greenville-
Spartanburg, South Carolina
www.erh.noaa.gov/er/gsp

This website offers text and graphical forecasts for Alexander, Avery, Caldwell, McDowell, and Mitchell Counties in North Carolina.

National Weather Service Forecast Office,
  Morristown, Tennessee
www.srh.noaa.gov/mrx

This website offers text and graphical forecasts for the Damascus, Virginia, region and all the Tennessee areas covered in the rides.

Ray's Weather Center
http://booneweather.com

This website provides up-to-the-minute weather observations from locations across the High Country, a live weather cam, and fearless forecasts by Ray Russell, an associate professor of computer science at Appalachian State University.

APPENDIX C
HIGH COUNTRY BICYCLE SHOPS

Adventure Damascus Bicycles
128 West Laurel Avenue
Damascus, Va. 24236
888-595-2453 or 276-475-6262
www.adventuredamascus.com

Beech Mountain Sports
325 Beech Mountain Parkway
Banner Elk, N.C. 28604
828-387-2795
www.beechmountainsports.com

Biking Buddies
137 Blevins Express Road
West Jefferson, N.C. 28694
336-246-7603

Boone Bike and Touring
899 Blowing Rock Road
Boone, N.C. 28607
828-262-5750

Cook's
West Park Shopping Center
North Wilkesboro, N.C. 28659
336-667-4121

Fuller's Action Cycles
9 North Main Street
Marion, N.C. 28752
828-652-5358
www.fullerscycles.com

Magic Cycles
140 South Depot Street #2
Boone, N.C. 28607
828-265-2211
www.magiccycles.com

New River Riders Bike Shoppe
208 East Stuart Drive
Galax, Va. 24333
877-510-2572 or 276-236-5900
www.newriverriders.com

Reef Dancer Dive Center
1607 Curtis Bridge Road
Wilkesboro, N.C. 28697
336-903-8747
www.reefdancerdiving.com

APPENDIX D
HIGH COUNTRY ROAD-CYCLING EVENTS

Visit NCDOT's statewide cycling-events calendar at www.ncdot.org/transit/bicycle/calendar for current dates and contact information on these and other North Carolina cycling events.

Assault on Mount Mitchell and Assault on Marion

This century ride, held each May, begins in Spartanburg, South Carolina. Sponsored by the Freewheelers of Spartanburg bike club, it is the granddaddy of the mountain endurance events. It runs from Spartanburg in the South Carolina foothills to the highest point in eastern America, the summit of Mount Mitchell. A 72-mile route from Spartanburg to Marion, North Carolina, is also offered. For more information, visit www.freewheelers.info/assault.html.

Beat Goes On

This event is held in October in Spruce Pine. A century ride amidst fall foliage, it boasts more than 6,600 feet of climbing. A 57-mile option with 4,280 feet of climbing is also available. The ride benefits the Spruce Pine Community Hospital Foundation. For more information, call 828-766-1750 or visit www.spchfdn.org.

Blood, Sweat and Gears

"Just Enough Pain" is the slogan for this 100-mile loop ride through the mountains of Watauga and Ashe Counties. A 56-mile option is also available. Blood, Sweat and Gears is held in June and originates in Boone. The route features more than 10,000 feet of climbing, including a steep slog up Snake Mountain. This well-supported ride benefits the disaster-relief fund of the Watauga County Chapter of the American Red Cross. It has won several Best Biking in America awards, including a well-deserved "Most Challenging" accolade in 1999. For more information, call 828-264-8226 or visit www.bloodsweatandgears.org.

Blue Ridge Brutal 100

Held in West Jefferson during August, this loop ride through the mountains of Ashe and Alleghany Counties is billed as a century, but it actually clocks in at a little over 105 miles. The route includes 27 miles of the Blue Ridge Parkway and a brutal climb up Three Top Mountain. A half-century option is available. The ride has earned several Best Biking in America awards and a mention in *Bicycling* magazine. For more information, call 336-246-4483 or visit http://asheciviccenter.com/brbrutal.html.

Blue Ridge Mountain Challenge

Held in Marion in late October, this hilly half-century ride includes 10 miles of the Blue Ridge Parkway and a blazing descent on N.C. 80. For more information, call 828-652-4240 or visit www.mcdowellnc.org/chamber/fallevents.htm.

Bridge-To-Bridge Incredible Challenge

This 100-miler, held in September, starts in the foothills at Lenoir and finishes atop Grandfather Mountain. Fourteen aid stations help riders cope with the challenging terrain. The scenic route includes the Yonahlossee Trail and the Linn Cove Viaduct section of the Blue Ridge Parkway. The last two miles on the access road to the top of Grandfather Mountain are beyond steep. For more information, call 800-468-7325 or visit www.caldwellcochamber.org/b2bpage.htm.

Burnsville Metric

This event is held in Burnsville during April. For more information, call 828-675-5132 or visit www.bicycleinn.com/BMMetric01.htm.

Mountain Glory Metric Century

Held in Marion in October, this 100K event features a challenging course and beautiful mountain scenery. After the ride, cyclists can join the festivities of the Mountain Glory Festival. For more information, call 828-652-6270.

Rhododendron Cycling Celebration

This two-day road-cycling festival, held in Spruce Pine during the month of June, offers a century, an 18-miler, and several rides in between. It coincides with nearby Bakersville's annual North Carolina Rhododendron Festival. For more information, call 828-688-2473 or visit www.bikewnc.com.

Rides Around Wilkes

This event is held in Wilkesboro in May. The Brushy Mountain Cyclists Club offers 25-, 40-, and 70-mile options through the foothills of Wilkes and Alexander Counties. Though its top elevation is only 2,200 feet, the 70-mile RAW route features a stout 6,300 feet of climbing, making this a good warmup for the Assault on Mount Mitchell, held later in May. For more information, visit http://ridesaroundwilkes.tripod.com.

Roan Moan

Moan you will during the steep century route or the metric-century alternative offered in this benefit ride, held in Bakersville during July. The 100-mile option loops through the Unaka Mountains on the North Carolina-Tennessee border and includes a memorable climb to Carver's Gap (elevation 5,512 feet) near Roan Mountain. Both routes finish with sweet descents back to Bakersville. For more information, call 828-688-9333 or visit www.bicycleinn.com/RoanMoanInfo.htm.

Rollin' Round the River Ride

Held in Wilkesboro in September, this relatively easy half-century follows the route of "The Happy Valley Tour" through the upper Yadkin River Valley. The ride benefits the Wilkes County Special Olympics cycling team. For more information, call 336-667-6836 or visit http://brushymtncyclists.tripod.com/id18.htm.

APPENDIX E
HIGH COUNTRY FESTIVALS AND EVENTS

An Appalachian Summer

This series of concerts and other cultural events is held in July at Appalachian State University in Boone, North Carolina, and other nearby sites. For more information, call 800-841-ARTS or visit www.appsummer.org.

Art in the Park

High-quality arts and crafts are displayed in Blowing Rock, North Carolina, on selected Saturdays from May through October. For more information, call 828-295-7851 or visit www.blowingrock.com.

Avery County Heritage Festival

This event takes place in Newland, North Carolina, during June. For more information, call 800-972-2183.

Brushy Mountain Apple Festival

This huge street festival in North Wilkesboro, North Carolina, held the first Saturday in October, celebrates the annual apple harvest. For more information, call 336-838-8662 or visit www.applefestival.net.

Christmas in July

This three-day festival in West Jefferson, North Carolina, celebrates the area's Christmas-tree growers. For more information, call 800-343-2743 or visit www.christmasinjuly.info.

Damascus Trail Days

This mid-May festival in Damascus, Virginia, celebrates the annual arrival of through-hikers attempting the 2,150-mile Appalachian Trail. More than 1,000 hikers participate in the hiker parade and talent show. For more information, call 540-475-3831 or visit www.traildays.com.

Merlefest

During the last weekend in April, Wilkesboro, North Carolina, hosts a massive four-day Americana music event on the campus of Wilkes Community College. The festival is named for Doc Watson's late son, Merle. An admission fee is charged. For more information, call 800-343-7857 or 336-838-6100 or visit www.merlefest.org.

Mountain Glory Festival

Those who attend this festival, held in Marion, North Carolina, in October, enjoy live entertainment from gospel and bluegrass to rock. Children's events are held, and vendors sell food and crafts. For more information, call 828-652-2215.

Mountain Heritage Festival

Held in Sparta, North Carolina, the last weekend in September, this event features mountain music, food, and crafts. For more information, call 800-372-5473.

North Carolina Rhododendron Festival

Bakersville, North Carolina, hosts this three-day festival in June. For more information, call 800-227-3912 or visit http://www.bakersville.com/rhod.html.

Old Boone Street Fest

This festival takes place in Boone the last Saturday in September. For more information, call 800-852-9506.

Old Time Fiddlers Convention

This event takes place in Galax, Virginia, the second weekend in August. An admission fee is charged. For more information, call 276-236-8541 or visit www.oldfiddlersconvention.com.

On the Square Arts and Crafts Festival

Those who come to Newland in July can enjoy a Friday-night street dance and a Saturday crafts show with more than 80 vendors. For more information, call 828-898-8755.

Overmountain Victory Trail Celebration

A Revolutionary War reenactment is conducted in Spruce Pine, North Carolina, in late September. For more information, call 800-227-3912.

Shady Valley Cranberry Festival

Crafts, food, music, rides, and cranberry-bog tours are featured at this festival on the grounds of historic Shady Valley School in Shady Valley, Tennessee. The event takes place the second full weekend in October. For more information, call 423-739-5077 or visit http://pages.preferred.com/~jcwc/cranberryfestival.htm.

Todd New River Festival

A "Ducky Derby," food, and mountain music are the staples at this festival, held in Todd, North Carolina, the second Saturday in October. For more information, call 336-877-1067.

Trade Days

People come to Trade, Tennessee, the last full weekend in June to dance, to witness moonshine making, to sample the apple butter, and more. For additional information, call 423-727-9511 or visit www.tradedaysfestival.com.

Valle Country Fair

Valle Crucis, North Carolina, hosts this festival of mountain music, arts, and crafts the third Saturday in October. For more information, call 800-852-9506 or visit www.vallecountryfair.org.

Woolly Worm Festival

This festival honors woolly worm larvae, which are reputed to predict the severity of the coming winter. A $1,000 cash prize goes to the winner of the Woolly Worm Race. The festival is held in Banner Elk, North Carolina, in mid-October. For more information, call 800-972-2183 or visit http://woollyworm.com.

BIBLIOGRAPHY

Anderson, J. Jay. *Wilkes County Sketches*. Wilkesboro, N.C.: Wilkes Community College, 1976.

Armstrong, Lance. *It's Not About the Bike: My Journey Back to Life*. New York: G. P. Putnam's Sons, 2000.

Ashe County Bicentennial Commission Historical Committee. *Rambling Through Ashe*. Jefferson, N.C.: Carolina Printing Co., 1976.

Bake, William A. *The Blue Ridge*. Birmingham, Ala.: Oxmoor Press, 1984.

Blackmun, Ora. *Western North Carolina: Its Mountains and Its People to 1880*. Boone, N.C.: Appalachian Consortium Press, 1977.

Bledsoe, Jerry. *Blue Horizons: Faces and Places from a Bicycle Journey Along the Blue Ridge Parkway*. Asheboro, N.C.: Down Home Press, 1993.

Ferguson, Thomas W. *Home on the Yadkin*. Winston-Salem, N.C.: Clay Printing Co., 1957.

Fields, Margaret, and Ida Phillips Lynch. *A Guide to Nature Conservancy Projects in North Carolina*. Durham, N.C.: The Nature Conservancy, N.C. Chapter, 2000.

Hallowell, Barbara G. *Mountain Year: A Southern Appalachian Nature Notebook*. Winston-Salem, N.C.: John F. Blair, Publisher, 1998.

Hometown Memories: Blue Ridge Tales. Conover, N.C.: Hometown Memories Publishing Co., 1996.

Hudson, Patricia L., and Sandra L. Ballard. *The Smithsonian Guide to Historical America: The Carolinas and the Appalachian States*. New York: Stewart, Tabori and Chang, 1989.

Lord, William G. *Blue Ridge Parkway Guide: Grandfather Mountain to Great Smoky Mountains National Park*. Birmingham, Ala.: Menasha Ridge Press, 1994.

Lord, William G. *Blue Ridge Parkway Guide: Roanoke to Grandfather Mountain*. Birmingham, Ala.: Menasha Ridge Press, 1994.

McDaniel, Lynda. *Highroad Guide to the North Carolina Mountains*. Winston-Salem, N.C.: John F. Blair, Publisher, 1998.

Moore, Warren. *Mountain Voices: A Legacy of the Blue Ridge and Great Smokies*. Winston-Salem, N.C.: John F. Blair, Publisher, 1988.

Noblitt, Phillip T. *A Mansion in the Mountains: The Story of Moses and Bertha Cone and Their Blowing Rock Manor*. Boone, N.C.: Parkway Publishers, 1996.

Orr, Douglas M., Jr., and Alfred W. Stuart. *The North Carolina Atlas: Portrait of a New Century*. Chapel Hill: University of North Carolina Press, 2000.

Reeves, Eleanor Baker. *A Factual History of Early Ashe County, N.C.* Dallas, Tex.: Taylor Publishing Co., 1986.

Rucker, John. *A Seasonal Guide to the Natural Year: A Month by Month Guide to Natural Events, North Carolina, South Carolina, Tennessee*. Golden, Colo.: Fulcrum Publishing, 1996.

Sakowski, Carolyn. *Touring the Western North Carolina Backroads*. Winston-Salem, N.C.: John F. Blair, Publisher, 1990.

Scheer, Julian, and Elizabeth McD. Black. *Tweetsie: The Blue Ridge Stemwinder*. Charlotte, N.C.: Heritage House, 1958.

Thompson, Roy. *Before Liberty*. Winston-Salem, N.C.: Piedmont Publishing Co., 1976.

Van Noppen, Ina W., and John J. Van Noppen. *Western North Carolina Since the Civil War*. Boone, N.C.: Appalachian Consortium Press, 1973.

INDEX

The author and publisher have made every effort to make this guide as accurate as possible. However, many things can change after a guide is published—roads may be improved or rerouted, facilities may close, etc.

We would appreciate your feedback concerning your experiences with this guide and suggestions for how it might be approved in future editions. Please send your comments via email to sakowski@blairpub.com or mail them to:

John F. Blair, Publisher
1406 Plaza Drive
Winston-Salem, NC 27103

You might also want to visit the author's website at http://blueridgebiking.tripod.com.

We will try to post any updated information on that site as we become aware of it.